God's Butterfly
Redefined For Purpose

God's Butterfly
Redefined For Purpose

Ornitha Danielle

Library of Congress Control Number: 2016909448

Published By: So Fyh Publishing Ink Inc., & Ornitha Danielle
E-mail addresses: danielle_taylor2006@yahoo.com
info@ornithadanielle.info
editor@sofyhmagazineonline.biz
Website: http://www.sofyhmagazineonline.com
Website: http://ornithadaniellesbooksdotinfo.weebly.com
Photo on the front of the book cover © Lee Taylor of So Fyh Photography
Book Cover: Ornitha Danielle and So Fyh Publishing Ink Inc.,
Editors/Proofreaders: So Fyh Publishing Ink Inc.
Content Editor: Lee Taylor
Proofreaders: Lee Taylor, Tara Woodley, and Vena Darling

CONTENTS

Dedication
Dear Reader
Acknowledgements
Introduction of Book
God's Butterfly
The Process of An Emerging Butterfly
My Dream Reality
Trying of Faith
The Silence In The Speech
Waking Up and Facing Reality
Let Go and Trust God
The Dance
The Power of The Scribal Prophet's Pen
Something To Think About
Understanding Your Kingdom Authority and Your Sphere of Influence
Greater Expectancy
You Are Destined For Greatness
You Are Royalty
Faithful
A Heart for Hollywood
You Have Been Equipped For The Battle
Heaven Reign
Know Your Worth
Man Down!
Hurt Issues Are A Heart Issus?
First Responder?
The Blossoming Rose
Your Light Should Not Be Hidden
Wounds Healed
A Community That Needs Healing
Brokenness To Wholeness
Walking In Purpose
Your Destiny Awaits
Loving The Beautiful Soul Within

Dream A Dream, A Poetic Dream....
A Remarkable Journey
Identity Revealed Through Intimacy
Once Upon A Time
Greater Expectancy
Use The Master's Keys
Signs of True and Real Maturity
Grandma You Are Loved
Waiting Patiently Wednesday... The Wisdom of God
But Seeing Through the Eyes of Christ
Transparent Moment
Growing Pains
Not the Church as Usual
My Soapbox For The Day!
Fond Memory
Prayer and Training are Essential for the Destination
Step of Faith into The Unknown Realm With God
I AM Poetry In Motion
Jesus Loves Me
What's Love Have To Do With It?
Do You Remember?
Living With No Regrets
My Pen
This Is My Roar
Still People
Our Fall
Just Be
Your Next Destination
Fairytales of Reality
Uncertainties
Never Forfeit
Levels & Stages of Healing
God's Plan
What He Requires?
War Silently
Un-blurred Vision
Wake Up
Reality Based Talk

Spiritual Prostitution
Remembrance
Daniel The Influencer
Stop It and Use Wisdom
Next Phase

Dedication

I dedicate this book to my husband Rodney Lee Taylor, Sr. Words couldn't describe how much your love and support has meant to me. Time has come yet again, another chapter in my life has been turned, but not without you.

I know that it can be difficult at times to see me write like nobody's business, but I am glad and thankful that God has shown you that it's not just something that I do, but that it's my calling to use my Scribal Pen and to legislate what I have been sent here to do. I so thank God for you! I love you for loving such imperfect person like myself, without barriers.

Your Loving Wife,

Ornitha

Dear Reader,

Once again I want to thank you for sowing into good ground and the creative work that God once again has allowed me the precious opportunity to share His with you. I never take anything that I required to do for the Kingdom of Heaven lightly. I pray that even as you continue to read that your will be ignited, inspired and loved as you digest the contents from this book.

In this creative work of words that spilled from my pen to paper, to flowing through your eye gates will bring such peace joy and happiness into your dwelling place. As with the last book **"A Portrait of Words, Divinely Speaking "** know that this book has been bathe in prayer. Remember to take hold of God's unchanging hand, and that if He can bring you to it, most certainly He take you through it, and bring you out.

May God continue to bless you, and know that you are blessed in your coming as well as your going. With this isn't just about writing a good book, to entertain others, but it a time to bring them to a place where they can meet the one God that is the creator of All things. To know that He wants to love you, teach and guide into your purpose and destiny. Because of who He is, you are. God bless you. You have a choice today and that is to LOVE!

Ornitha Danielle

Acknowledgements

First and foremost I have to give honor to my Lord and Savior Jesus Christ! Without Him none of this would be possible. He's the reason that I am sharing the messages in this book with you. I don't take any of this lightly and I do consider it an honor that God would call me His Scribal Prophet and uses me the way that he so desires. In this portion of this book, it is only befitting that I acknowledge God. The bible tells us in Proverbs 3:5-6 *Trust in the LORD with all thine heart; and lean not unto thine own understanding. In all thy ways acknowledge him, and he shall direct thy paths.*

To everyone that has allowed this book to enter their homes, minds and heart, I want to thank you for allowing my writings to be apart for that experience. To my family and friends thank you for your prayers and support. This has been yet another journey with Holy Spirit to even begin such a task, but one that I don't do alone.

Introduction of Book

Transparency moment (I am just kind of in my feelings a bit today.) Sometimes it's okay to cry in the midst of your journey, when the road becomes a bit difficult. I know that I can become a bit emotional at times, here I am learning how to BE OKAY with me, and even more so comfortable with my own skin, my own voice and most importantly my own creativity. I never felt or ever thought that I was good enough... There seemed to always be some type of expectation to perform in some way or fashion.

I've found myself hiding and afraid to allow the True Beauty within myself to come through, afraid of what others may feel or think, not being me. My personality... those that know; me will truly understand what I am saying. No, I haven't be pretending, but its one of things where you are in a crowd of people but you still feel alone. That has been the story of my life...

This book that I have been working on God's Butterfly has really stirred up some deep hidden things that I had completely forgotten about... Holy Spirit truly knows how to get stuff out of you. I've found myself moving and operating in so many things and I had no clue, who I was, why I was doing, or how I had even obtained the gifts that God had blessed me with. I never saw myself as a writer, poet, His Scribal Prophet...

I am truly blessed that God loves me just that much to call me His own. As, we all know with everything in life, it is a process, and with God's grace which is sufficient enough for me, I am overcoming daily. Not in my strength but in his strength. No longer living in the areas of others' hopes and dreams for me, but in the ones that God has for me, and the life that I am living today, I want and strive to be better than I was the days before. Living a life pleasing to the Lord, and basking in his love for me. It's okay to allow God to love you during your journey

God's Butterfly

Mere essence of beauty that He holds
My existence has been foretold
The gentle grace that glides in the air
Wisdom a floats the majesties of God's love to share

Unique in colors, I move, but there's no speech
God knows of what's untold and his ways are beyond my reach
Infancy is the start, as I am always upon HIS heart
Flight is just the beginning, not my ending, flying with purpose and
filled with destiny

The joy and laughter is here in and between
Knowing that His fabric of love, dances in me midstream
Crafted to display all of God's miracle, signs and wonders, in my
wings I spread, for my Failures I do ponder, knowing that your love
does cover

Tranquility is amiss
Dreams are abound
No longer a frown, because I am found
Brightly I am that I fly to see, that Heaven is my final destiny
My purpose will not die, because you are with me
Laying awake at night, as my soul is lifted high

Distance is between all of my heaven's dreams
Waiting to meet you face to face,
My God, my very love has shifted through time and space
Your eyes are always on me as my heartbeats for you
I am love by GOD through and through

I am God's Butterfly
Keeping me warm and your love
That is my cocoon from above
There's nothing that keeps you from me,

Ornitha Danielle

YOU are the perfect love that a girl like me can get use too

No matter where I go, you are guiding my very steps
I am God's Butterfly…
To fly free among the stars and trees
I am God's Butterfly…

Lord are you watching your daughter as the winds are beneath my wings?
I am God's Butterfly…
To glide and twirl and dance as you direct,
You are creating me to be perfect

I am God's Butterfly… What a dream to be
That you created the very essence of ME!
I missed the butterfly net so many times,
That you said that I am to allow my light to shine

The Process of An Emerging Butterfly

As I am sitting at this computer screen, thinking and writing about the very cycle and the process of a butterfly. How much it has to endure to be it can become what it's destined to be. To look at the process, that it starts out. It blesses me to know that even in the beginning it's an egg, and will become the butterfly.

Sometimes we can get very excited or frustrated about the many stages that we often have to go through, but if we wait and allow the process and maturity to come we can see what is being done in the midst.

Regardless of what the situation or circumstance are we can't rush the process. The other side is sometimes others may want to assist you, helping you breakout of that safety place of the cocoon can very well hurt you. Because if you never gain the strength to fly, to spread your wings, you'll not fulfill, you can't get to that place you need to be.

The struggle is needed, I believe not only does it teaches how to stay in the war, and give it everything to stay alive. I'm very certain that in the stage of fighting for your rightful place, it causes the very things inside to come forth **BOLD**!

I am reminded of my times when I wanted to not even fight anymore, I was so in place trying to come forward, but the **STRUGGLE** was so **GREAT**! It would have been easier to not fight anymore.

However, God begin to show me, how much my survival was, and to know that no matter what others thought, His thoughts toward me existence was far than I could see. Before we can even see the beautiful colors on the wings of a butterfly, we have to see the process of the struggle.

Think of it like this... from the very moment you were born there was process that your time in the womb. I know that's a lot to think

about, during that process at the start of a new month, your development changes. If your process or development is interrupted it can harmful and even life threatening. I'm saying that is the case always, but just sometimes the situation is very critical and there's a time when help is needed.

My Dreams Reality

If there's ever a moment in time that I was truly indeed sure of IS
THIS
Could I have dreamed it, or thought about it a million times
Only to realize that it's only what you make it
Having the Faith to move the impossible mountains that stand in my
path, Understanding God's plans are the best way
No longer trying to PUSH against the
Leading into what's so uncomfortable
It seems like a lifetime of endless cycles
Fearing to step out of the comfort zone
Into the great unknown

Time passes, seasons change and things get old
Amazing times of release for this new place of expectancy
I am seeing, now realizing and the magnitude of what is to become
of this journey
The very words that bleed from my pen,
Will tell of my struggles in overcoming and that I live to write again

I did the impossible with God; I lived my dreams a thousand times
I have cried a many tears, and yet God still took care of me
My life was written on a scroll and penned by the finger of God
I'm here because of what was in His heart

God's essence of His character and
It is profound that I have yet to touch, but it's at arm's reach,
Because He loves just that much
His ways are hard to wrap this mindsets around
The value that He has place inside of
His children can't be carbon copied,
We're unique in design, our image is divine, and we are one of a
kind

Sweet melodies, quiet whispers, and soft footsteps
Can be delightful sounds in our midst,

13

Speechless nothing; no more what ifs will be voiced, no more

placing it in this earth's atmosphere

Never again will this opportunity be missed
I've dreamed many dreams,
Some I have yet to see... trust me I do record what is shown to me
I am leaving behind my legacy
With my pen, my ink on paper
I pen

Trying of Faith

As, I am sitting here working on a few projects I began to start thinking about Faith. I am so blown away by how much our Faith level is tried & **TESTED!** For far so long we have seen and heard about the many situations and circumstances throughout the word of God, where many of the people had to rely on their Faith in God to believe the impossible. Then the scripture that comes to mind is this in the book of

Hebrews 11:6 (CJB) And without trusting, it is impossible to be well pleasing to God, because whoever approaches him must trust that he does exist and that he becomes a Rewarder to those who seek him out.

I can't help but think that we have to move from a place of relying on our human abilities and our educated intellect when it comes to things of God. I have learned a many of things that have now been torn down because of my own belief and the opinions of others, and not what God is saying and what he has said before.

When you get into a place where Holy Spirit beings to breath life, and that understanding, and revelation to His Word. Talk about **DELIVERANCE!** I have found so much peace, freedom and knowing that God will do everything possible to bring us what we need, but the key here is **FAITH!!**

The Silence In The Speech

There are so many things that give off sound
An old saying "that's music to my ears"
The blowing of the wind on a cool autumn night
Tunes that escaped the expanding lungs of the hummingbird
Knowing that these things are musical instruments in God's hands

The sound of thunder, but the flickers of lighting that doesn't
produce a sound, but does the eye move faster than the two?
The lost souls that cry out from the world's harsh and bitter pain
Lord, what has become of The Silence In The Speech
Do we just pretend that we don't hear, but this tugging at my heart,
as I try to cast down the thoughts of fear?

Father can't you not hear?
For goodness sakes, why are so many dying from the spirit of fear?
Again I ask, what's the problem here?
Do we not believe for what we ask, or did we just forget about the
reason that the veil was torn
So many speak of the many messages that you gave, and right to this
day
Help us even now, as you are ordering our steps, because we need
you more each and every day.

Tears plummet to the ground, but does it give off sound?
We walk along the path that has been set for us
No longer climbing mountain, but I've learned to speak to it, and it
moves
What more should I do, my faith has grown, but sometimes its very
hard to see
God you have always proven your unconditional love for me

Your covenant I thank you for, my access to heaven's door
Rainbows remind me of your promises of what you said
Your word brings life to my bones, oh how I long to be with you,
I will continue what you started in me, and do all that I can so that

you will get the glory
Do we just pretend that we don't hear?
Or do be pretend that we don't see
That way it doesn't happen or it's happening
To see your ocean and be reminded of the flood back in the days of
Noah
The things that I see I can't help but to think of all
That you created with your hand for us to enjoy
And yet we act as if it's not enough, you bleed on a cross for us;
indeed that was
The Silence In The Speech

You laid down your life for all humanity, and that was
The Silence In The Speech
Down to hell you went and took back your authority
Your blood overcame the coldness of the cross and burial

To show your love that you freely gave
Your love still spoke as you hung from the stake,
As you released your spirit into the hands of your Father
Who art in Heaven and hallowed be thy name
The ground began to quake
What has been done to God's only begotten son?
Who had sinned none

Waking Up And Facing Reality

I am sitting looking at my screen on my computer. There are so many things that I could do, but I am having a little moment, all in my feelings. I decided to have a little down time today, watched a few movies, and I have been reminded of the things. I use to dream about, and thought about as child and to actually be living out loud in many of them. All I ever wanted in my life was to be heard. I can remember when I was school all I did was write. I lived in creativity it was a very safe place for me.

Nothing else made any sense to me at all. I think my life took a turn by the time I was in 6th grade. I had to write a book report for English, but I think back then it was called Language Arts. Times have truly changed. There was never a moment that I didn't have a notepad, pen or pencil with, oh not to mention a book. My journey started very early, I became an avid reader... I read **EVERYTHING**!

If there were words I read it... I also keep a diary... the cute ones with the keys, but I wrote so much that I had to switch to a journal, then from there it spiral notebooks... I think that so many times, we struggle to find ourselves, or be defined by the things that we do, or have achieved, there all fine, but there's so much more. I think I spent most of the time, being told what I could not do, or have, or whether my ideas where good or not. That's no place for anyone to live...

Then the unthinkable happened.... the very thing that I found comfort in was stripped... My diary/ journal was discovered... when I about between 12 and 14, and from there I never wrote again! I didn't start writing again until I was about 18 or so... I had moved out on my own. I've done my very best at the end of the day, living the best life that I can possibly live, and treating God's people with Love and respect, regardless of where they are in their walk with the Lord. Some maybe a little stronger than others, but the fact is this.... Am I exemplifying the Love God in what I do? Lord, keep me in place of humility, love and have compassion for your people. Father, forgive me where I have failed to do so, whether it was unknown to me, that

I missed it. I want to be pleasing to you, I want to represent you, and I was sent here, by you to do a great work. For every soul that I will encounter, that I don't miss the opportunity to share your love.... Show me your Glory; heal me with your word. Prayer is very essential and its God's will for us to live a life in this way... Pray without ceasing. When we fail to follow this we become weak, and at times can be bait for the tricks, plots and plans that the enemy have to throw along the path. If we would just simply give **THANKS** and Pray, we can begin to see the things in and around us change.

From a firsthand account of what that looks like, although seeing things with the natural eye, would cause anyone to become alarmed, worried, frustrated, **BUT SEEING THROUGH THE EYES OF CHRIST**!! That spiritual eye and having the understanding that **HIS PLANS**, are for Good and not evil that is over in the book of *Jeremiah 29:11...* I'm thankful that I grew up with a fear of God, I longed to understand and to become more and more like The Father in Heaven that created me for a time such as **NOW**!

When I learned to stop compromising, justifying and competing with the world, my vision began to change. No longer walking in the scope of Tunnel Vision, but having a new vision, one that is better than 20/20, seeing as God sees gives me hope, and not an illusion as the world would refer to it. Let's not put the **PRO** in Procrastination. This problem can lead to other problems, whether it's in business, school or hobbies. If we want to be taken serious in what we do, we have to learn how to have that follow through type of mindset. Finish what you start! Never take on more if you're not completing what you already have. Zeal can have us starting off to a great start; the thrill of excitability, and once that comes down, that along with the other things end up incomplete. Revisit those things again... Don't be robbed of your ability, by the inability to move past **PRO**crastination. Put a stop to it, your future is depending on it.

Let Go and Trust God

I know this maybe a bit lengthy, but I pray that it blesses someone. A lot of times many of us have been told to get out there in the world and make all the money you can, but never are we told to pursue God like we pursue worldly things. I'm not saying that you can't have great success, but we must want God more! I have been guilty of trying to get my hustle on... I'm about dem dollars, Paper chaser, get your grind on, making this cheese, counting my bank or capital! Gotta get out here to this easy money! Trust me, it was there.

That's what I knew and learned how to do, and I was good at it. I did get into things where I felt I could get **RICH** quick deals; if that wasn't the biggest eye-opener ever. Then all of sudden that became my god, (transparency moment) everything around me began to crumble...This was truly not God, in any of that... Now I pursue God, **MATURITY**!! God wasn't impressed by any of what I was doing or had grown to doing. (One thing is certain, God's love will **ALWAYS REMAIN**)

Even when you lose things, jobs, careers, income. God is still God! Took me awhile to get that, then to really understand it. God began to teach me how to live off of what He supplies and provides. As, I began to follow God and use the very things that He placed inside of me... That alone has been my strength. I stopped putting my trust, time and energy into those things, and I begin to allow God to remove that hustle type of mentality and grind mode out of my system, and far from my vocabulary.

No matter how many jobs, career opportunities, degrees, certifications, places you go, or the people you meet along the way... **NUMBER 1 PRIORITY MUST BE GOD**! *Mark 8:36(CJB)* 36 Indeed, what will it benefit a person if he gains the whole world but forfeits his life? In the book of *Philippians 3:8-9 (CJB)* 8 Not only that, but I consider everything a disadvantage in comparison with the supreme value of knowing the Messiah Yeshua as my Lord. It was because of him that I gave up everything and regards it all as garbage, in order to gain the Messiah 9 and be found in union with him, not having any righteousness of my own based on legalism, but having that righteousness which comes through the Messiah's faithfulness, the righteousness from God based on trust.

The Dance

As my memory is a vivid as the sun
It's so hard to believe that so much has been done
Not realizing that it could never be undone
To wait aimlessly for the dance that I never had
I could run around in circles and look at the broken promises
And the books of empty and unfulfilled dreams
Distance in my heart and unspoken realities
To see and imagine a time and space
Of what a vision of what love would look like today
Standing in a mirror that has seemed to crumble into a million and one pieces
I walked backwards into a corner
Never to understand this sound of the rumbling thunder
Slowly I rocked back and forth
Hearing that faint knock at the door

I jump for joy only to be disappointed again
You took the last breath that I held in
Once again I let myself believing in a fairy-tail that never came true
Then I realized that all you cared about was you
Who would protect me from this cold and cruel world?
What matter most was this helpless and broken little girl
I extended my hand for what should have been my first dance
But instead it was disappointment that I experienced at your hand

The music begins to play everyone moves to the floor
There I am standing alone
Without a dance partner of my own
In the background of the music
I could hear my soul cry
That every minute that little girl inside me died
Everything that I'd hoped and imagine would be
Somehow turned out to be such misery

I tried everything I could think of to get you to notice me

Nothing seemed to work,
It was always something else that had your attention
Did I mention that I could scream at the top of my lungs?
Deaf ear you became
In the midst of my pain
My self-worth, self-esteem, no pun intended and pray none taken
The self that I never knew
Because part of me
That got me here
Never taught me how to love me

Alone to face a world that only loves its own
I realize that I didn't fit in nor did I belong
Hurt and frustrated by this event called life
Never in years did I think that I would step into a role,
That one day I would be someone's wife?
I didn't know which way to turn or go
I never followed the yellow brick road
I've prayed time and time again for God call me home
In this huge world alone
Drowning in a sea of tears, trying to move forward for all these years
Only to grieve over a loss of bond that never took place
I'm often told about what was before
That part of memory has faded

Funny thing though I don't really recall
All I can remember is the scariness of that doll
There are only a few instances in my life that are happy to me
When I fell down and scraped my knee
You picked me up and carried me
What you said was it will be okay,
Let me make it better and dry your tears away
That scar still remains until this day
That was a lifetime ago… but when I look at now,
I can't help but smile
Each time I needed you, I never got my hopes up,
Because it would be the same thing again and again
So much has happened in my life that you missed out on

We're like two strangers meeting for the first time
When two different worlds collide
It's hard to believe that I am apart of you
How could you not be there?
You were my world
I thought I was your world
You've always been mine
In my eyes you could do no wrong
One thing I was sure of you always breaking my heart

First man that daughter loves is her father
When that changed things where never the same
Moving forward in this pattern of life
I have revisited this place before and deliverance would come
Doing what I saw, I would break and run

I ran from everything dreams, relationships, jobs and more
I even ran away from the one that loves me the most
Until one day, I couldn't take it anymore...
I surrender...
This is way too much for me to bare...

Then He knocked on my heart,
And extended his hand and helped me from my knees
I ran into the open arms of the one that has me
In the palms of his hands
The one that loves me unconditionally,
That loves me, comforts and guides me
God is the one that wrote down the plans for me
He told me that he was preparing me for purpose and destiny
Even though my "what" is visible now this will not be my end
I've learned to trust in the one that has made time for me, the one
who now calls me friend.

The Power of The Scribal Prophet's Pen

When you are walking in obedience and there's a word from the Lord to release, do you the enemy will do everything that he can within his power to stop that word from going forth. However that word must be released... I can only speak for me... I have held onto words for months, years, and weeks and don't you know God still had me release it? What's interesting is this... when you are faced with roadblocks and distractions nothing will stop the **POWER OF THE SCRIBAL PROPHET'S PEN!**

You might say what if a person isn't going to receive the word? Well chances are either that word is coming to correct and they already know it, and they don't want to hear what you have to say...

Oh but guess what? Nothing stops you from writing it down. Just because they don't want hear it, doesn't make it invalid. It's not you that they reject...it is **JESUS CHRIST**. See when we are connected to Him, we tend to feel and hear the heartbeat of God, what He feels when we reject him.

There was some many years ago that God begin to send me out to say a few things... what I found very interesting was this... I had to release a word to someone... and don't you know that the person said to me was this... I will only receive the good part of the word, but the rest I don't want. Bewildered in my look, I was like where do they do that at? That shows only shows immaturity on their part.

Ornitha Danielle

Something To Think About

Why is it that Joseph in the book of Matthew when he received a dream and the angel of the Lord telling him not to be afraid about taking Mary as his wife, that what she was carry is indeed that of Holy Spirit. Now when we have these certain dreams the first thing we say that's the enemy?

Even reading over the part in Luke where the angel once again came and spoke to Zachariah, giving him his punishment for not believing what was said... I had this talk with another sister in the Lord, and her response was he was put on mute... I mean he was rendered silent, saying that he will be like that until it has been fulfilled. Can you imagine that happening today? Could we begin to see God move more if we would stop trying to figure out his ways?

Walk A Little While Longer

Never make excuses for how God made you; stand in that place where God plants you, there will be a moving of things for the greater in your life. It is time to stand in the authority that God has given you, be not moved by the thoughts, ways and looks of men. Stand on the foundation that was already prepared for you.

There's a call to be Holy! Don't fall into the plans, traps, or tricks of the enemy. You have the authority to bind and loose, God has given you access to all that is needed. This is a call to **NOT COMPROMISE** no matter who it is! I hear the Lord saying, I am about to rearrange some things in your midst, I'm cutting off that is causing you to retreat.

A lot of times people tend to hide behind their own mess and want to blame others for their shortcomings and hang-ups which at times can be true for the most part, but there's also a point when WE have to say **ENOUGH IS ENOUGH**. With 2016 just moments away!

You have to decide how you will start today and the days to come; being a better **YOU**! Everyday, I am working and walking out difficulties in my life! Some of them are harder to overcome, but with God's help I will get there! God is truly a deliverer, no more false realities of seemingly like; I have it all under control, because I'm a work in progress... I am clay that is yet in the potter's hand that remains on His wheel for His purpose.

Oftentimes I am having these conversations with God about how I can be a better person, meaning to be a better servant to His people? What else do I need to die to, why does this still bother me? After seeking Him and staying in God's face for the answer, even though I didn't get it right away, but the answer came. When a person can truly minister to your soul without condemnation and point you back into the face of God and your spirit rises, talk about rejoicing!

Edification! Edification! Here is where you are standing face to face

27

with yourself and all of these emotions come flooding back to your mind?

Now it's time to sort through and deal with it... I have over the years grown accustom to compartmentalizing issues? Please don't act like you don't know what that is... Yeah! I would place things in their places, what I was willing to deal with and how I wanted to deal with it on my own time. One day I was sitting alone in my spare time, doing what I do best is write.

You Cannot Rush The Process

At some point in our lives "WE" have to take "**FULL**" responsibility for the "**CHOICES WE MAKE**". It's like this... picking up the pieces and keeps it moving. True enough if you keep running into a **BRICK** wall, guess what "**WHY KEEP RUNNING INTO A BRICK WALL**? Did it ever occur that there's another way of getting around it? Go around or climb over it or take it down brick by brick. I like to look at it like this... in my own life... If something keeps reoccurring in my life. It's time to deal with it!

In order to experience truly healing, deliverance and peace, you have to go through the process. That is the very thing... For example take a woman begin pregnant, although she's going through the process and **ALL** that goes alone with it... can't speed up the process. There are some serious consequences having a baby too soon. We have to go through the same process of being set **FREE**!

 Some things are truly out of our control, but others...(deep sigh) For instance it how we choose to respond to it, we can blow up, ignore, or have temper tantrum (which gets you nowhere) (signs of maturity) or we can take the matter to God in prayer.

You can lay out the blueprint to build a house, but it up to the builder to follow it. So when you end up with a shower in the kitchen... (**LOL**) The builder deviated from the plans. We can't allow what others do to get us off course, one thing is certain... If God said it, **TRUST** it will happen. God always has his way.

Understanding Your Kingdom Authority and Your Sphere of Influence

Understanding your Kingdom authority and your sphere of influence in the Kingdom of Heaven! So often time's people of God tend to become more and more **BUSY** at being **BUSY**! And as a result: Not effective in their assignment(s), due to the loss of details, lack of follow-through and disobedience!

It's ever so important to write down **ALL** the details to what is being given to you, if you have questions, I am sure that making your request made known, that the answer(s) that you're seeking God will truly answer them in **HIS** timing. Be about Kingdom Building and building up the people!

Greater Expectancy

When you are given clear instructions to go into a certain direction in life, nobody was there with you in the private time with the Lord, when He spoke. **ALWAYS** listen to God. If you move away from that plan or path that was shown you chaos can enter into your midst, **DISTRACTIONS** or you will get off focus and out of alignment; to what God has for your life.

Sometimes situations are stumbling blocks that would cause you to step out of character, or hinder the move of God, only out of frustration, but I want to encourage you today.... Move forward according to the plans of God, yes your plans do matter, just make sure that you seek God.

It's very important to be **OBEDIENT** to the call and the anointing that has been placed upon your life. Either you can move too fast, and miss it or you can move too slow and miss it. Learn to know the voice of God for yourself, from your own voice, and **STOP TALKING SOOOOO MUCH** to **OTHERS**, that have no clear direction or can't hear and trust God for themselves.

Learn how to pray and seek God until HIS peace comes. I will say this, there has been a many times when I know that God has told me to move, and run for my life and I did just that! If I hadn't done it, I would not be writing this message today. Its time to stop allowing others to pull from you, without being poured back into; it's time to be replenished.

If you can trust God for your life, then you can trust him to take care of **YOU**, and those things that concern you as well. God wants us to prosper as our soul prospers it's time to move into a new season of **EXPECTANCY!!!** To do **GREATER THINGS FOR THE KINGDOM OF GOD!!!**

You Are Destined For Greatness

It's sometimes somewhat comical when you realize that the enemy: just don't know when to stop. The tactics neither intimidates me, but I will continue to handle it in my prayer closet. One thing is for sure regardless how we tend to feel or react to a thing, have the **HUMILITY** to submit that unto the Lord. Survivor of what they enemy tried to do in my life, by direct or indirect means.

Truth shows that as I keep standing and not moving my position to that which could cause me my salvation, or will cause me to forfeit a blessing. I chose God every day. I know where all my help comes from. And the point that I can't compromise my walk, the destiny, or purpose to pursue my **FLESH**. I will continue to stand on God's word, for what is right! Not to the point of what feels okay at the moment. I pray that you will allow God into those places that would cause you to question that you are, and what God has for you.
Be it as it may, only what is done for God will last. Seeking anything other than the Kingdom is in direct violation to God's word. I am just saying... It's right there in Black and White. At the end of this life's journey I would have accomplished everything that God wrote in his word concerning me. Neither do I stand to accuse, but sin is exposed for it is... My prayer is that I keep a heart that is submitted before God, and walk according to the precepts that he's already set for me.

This is a daily walk, as **I DIE** to my ways of doing and thinking that I am always correct, however, what has been revealed in my time of study is only Holy Spirit. I rejoice in my trials tribulations, and my sufferings, because here I am strengthening to walk through it with God's help, and his Love that truly covers me. In this hour we have to take the very authority that God has given us and learn to exercise it... meaning put it to use! Thank God for those that come to do you harm, but pray for them. There's a time for everything, and sometimes we do our best fighting in the spirit, sometimes we have to remove ourselves from a situation in order to see the mighty hand of God.

You Are Royalty

Transparency Moment... As I am about to get my day started, I begin to feel very overwhelmed all of sudden, wasn't sure why at all. So I asked God what's wrong did I miss something, did I move in a way that I shouldn't, did I not say something when I should have, or did I speak too soon, please what is it Lord?

So I just sit here looking at this screen and like Lord, I can't today, I just can't today. He said "I'm birthing so much in right now, that you can today"! The area in which you walk in Creatively, Instructionally and Administratively is about to OVERTAKE YOU! So, as I just brace myself, shake me my head and let out the deepest sigh... Lord, why is it so hard, it seems like the more that I try to just be me, relax, and let it go, nothing is working? I am just a believer of what God has to say, and what He's doing... prayer does change things. Learning how to BE... I love me, and everything that God placed in me.

Sometimes it gets very hard for me to walk away from situations and circumstances that ONLY PRODUCE DEATH! I love God's truth, and sometimes it really hurts, but when you are a seeker of truth and fellowship with Him, the truth will make you free. We can't get to a place where we are blinded by the cares of this world, things or people. I love that God is RE-Writing my story every day, and I am thankful for everything that He is doing in me and through me.

I am at new place in my journey and I never would have thought that I, would be doing what I am doing right at this very moment in time (I JUST GAVE BIRTH). I have to say that we can allow fear 80% of the time, to restrict what God is trying to birth in us. I can only speak for myself. I have given so much of myself, to be of service to others... I know that I am a servant and never had a problem in doing so... but when that becomes a place of bondage, and place of lack for you and those that you wish to help.

It's time to re-evaluate what you are doing and if God said it in the beginning, or the season is just up. We can stay so far past or date of expiration on an assignment.

It is time to move on... For years, I have been in this place... My pastor asked me recently... what is God doing in you, what is God saying to you, where are you spiritually. Where was I in the word, and how was God moving in my life?

When I say that my pastor is ALL of That!! She is truly a WOG that walks, talks and lives what she teaches... loves people and will walk with you as you are coming to that place of wholeness. I have been in the book of Esther and Ruth which seems like forever, but I can't move from there. It's a remarkable journey. The Beauty of Holiness, and the Unfolding Beauty of Righteousness

Not one person has all of the answers, but this book that I am still adding the final touches to, and my alone time with the Lord, the teachings that has come from this process. I am about moved to tears, but it's not tears of sadness, but of BREAKING-THROUGH the COCOON! I have been travailing in the midst of it.... PHYSICALLY, MENTALLY, SPIRITUALLY, AND EMOTIONALLY.

I never thought that in all my life that having your HEARTBROKEN so that God can mend the diseased portions of it. I am still believing God to complete what He started, I am still believing the promises that He made to me, I am still believing that every word that God sent to me concerning me, is going to happen. Just a few days ago, I was in a tough battle... let me say this. Warfare is no joke...

Faithful

Divinely Speaking: **ARISE GENERATION EXTRAORDINARY**!! From where I read, and pray this is a new year of many things ahead... Looking for **NEW THINGS! NEW MOVES OF GOD, NEW REVELATIONS, NEW! NEW! NEW**!

As much as I try to do, the more God pulls me to come even deeper, as I have been praying and seeking God to understand this new journey; that I am in, this place of dying to my flesh in greater ways that I couldn't have even imagined.

My place is between the porch and the altar. I am reminded that I have to keep myself in a place to hear from God, and the intimacy with God is where I find my strength. I am not here of my own doing, but that of what God has placed in me since the beginning of this foundation.

Lord father, fill me even more of you, give me more of your spirit, your love, and your understanding, your character in this life that you've given me. Bless us lord in our search and understanding of your will for our lives, that we're not mislead, or stumble and our faith grows, as well as our service to you.

Open up your word to us, teach us your ways, and precepts that we will get in line, and walk according to what you've said throughout the word. Continue Oh Lord, may your perfect will be done in the lives of your people. Father help us to sit-down long enough to listen to what the spirit of the Lord is saying. More discernment is needed in this season... God uncover what is hidden in Jesus mighty name.

A Heart for Hollywood

Pondering Thought...

Sorry this maybe a little long, but I have to say this.

It's really something when you think about how far television shows, music, and the ways to communicate have changed. Whatever happened to the wholesome shows that dealt with issues, like **STDs** (Safe Sex), drinking and driving (**MADD Mothers Against Drunk Driving**), teen pregnancy, drug use/saying no to drugs, date rap, how to deal with racial injustice among **ALL** communities, teen suicide and other pressing issues? What happened to the shows that promoted family unity, getting a better education? The family structure as a whole... when sitting down at dinner to talk about what everyone's day was like.

Call it what you may, although the world is advancing through the ways of media and technology we can't be so blind that we fail to reach those that are lost. Sometimes my heart breaks when I hear about those childhood actors and singers that many of us grew up watching on television or even buying their music, to witness their downfall. I was a huge Michael Jackson fan; in 2009, when he died it was such an upsetting time for many.

I actually cried, when I heard the news... no matter the many things that people said that Michael Jackson did, we all still love him, his music, his videos, maybe even how strange he may have been. Not knowing all the details but to understand that another soul has left.

As, much as they are idolized all over the world, we have to really, really, really pray for them! I know we can see so much circulating all of over the Internet, concerning their lifestyles, what they do and whom they do it with. We can't forget they have a soul and God loves them just as much as He loves you.

Regardless of how we may feel in our mind about an individual and their choice of lifestyle remember they are also God's children. I'm so thankful that God never treated me like the sinner, but always showed me love and compassion, no matter what I did or didn't do.

We all have wilderness and desert places that we are walking out everyday, overcoming it everyday. Each day we get a little bit better than we were the day before. Sometimes we as people can place others and ourselves on these pedestal until one day we actually see the real person.

I've shared this in some of my previous post. Know me by the spirit, and know that if you're always looking at my flesh, my flesh man will always tend to disappoint you. I'm generally am a pretty cool person to myself at least. I try to handle everyone's feelings they way I would want my feelings handled and no I'm not acting all weird or anything, but I guess that's the compassionate side of me. Remember that God loves us all, and he gave us instructions on how to treat one another. If we can get on one accord and be the light to those that do walk in darkness, not to take advantage of them, but to be there to witness, pray, comfort and speak into their lives, as Holy Spirit would have you to.

You Have Been Equipped For The Battle

Sometimes I have to sit back and knowing that alone I never fight a battle unequipped, God wouldn't send one of His own to the frontline without tools and weapons to defeat whatever giant/mountain that is standing in the way. Even David, was equipped with a staff in his hand, a slingshot and five smooth stones, that he placed into his bag, he was ready for fight!

1 Samuel 17:40 40 (CJB) Then he took his stick in his hand and picked five smooth stones from the riverbed, putting them in his shepherd's bag, in his pouch. Then, with his sling in his hand, he approached the P'lishti.

No physical amour visible to the eye, he stood up against a giant several times his size, who had a helmet, breastplate, sandals, shield and sword? All things are possible when you know whom you serve. It doesn't matter what the situation looks like or hard you may think it may, or could be.... If you go in a mind... that **NO WEAPON FORMED AGAINST SHALL PROSPER**!! (Isaiah 54:17)

Heaven Reign

Every once in awhile you have to let go of the things that don't even deserve a moment's notice. Eviction notices are being sent out. I am going to have going to have peace! Anything coming less than that, it has to go! When you begin to see things through untainted glass, how much more clearly does it need to get? (PEACE IS MINE) God is the Prince of Peace!

Believe what the spirit of the living God is saying about your very situation, some things we do have jurisdiction over exercise that authority, with that begin said walk in the beautiful destiny that God has purposed for your life, not something else someone has said has to be. Knowing of God and having an intimate relationship with Him... There is a huge difference. Fear is tactic that causes people to behave in undignified ways. Mind control and manipulation are devices that they enemy uses... witchcraft is not of God.

Remember to grab hold to ALL of your dreams and visions, those are God's hidden messages to you when you are the most still and quiet enough to receive His revelation of truth concerning the plans for the future that is ahead of you for your journey and life ahead. Jeremiah 29:11

Set your eyes upon the Glory of the Father who is the beginning and the end of ALL things. Come let us reason together for a common cause and purpose and that being the love of God for one another. God is love, the lifter of our heads and our present help in the times of adversity. Much more exposure in this hour, but don't fear for God is with us and the government will be on His shoulders. As loud as the enemy tries to be, we have armies of angelic beings that war on our behalf and with us.

Raise the bar of intercession. God's will is going to be done. We must know the will of God. Reconciliation is coming! God has his people stationed everywhere and in every situation. So don't think that your concerns have gone unheard. Remember your own war rooms... preparing, positioning, and purposeful prayer in this hour has to be strategic and executed with a razor sharp precision. It's time to develop a prayer plan of action.

I see watchmen standing at the gates... (Gatekeepers) and on the walls (Watchmen On The Walls.) The hours are long, there's no gap in between shifts. It's a linking prayer watch... I see plenty of pens moving frantically legislating orders on behalf of their KING!

Know Your Worth

I pray that this helps someone... I have received tons of messages from people asking me if I am okay? I had no idea that what I share was helping anyone... I just share what God would have me to share.

This has been over the years and where I am now, I have the biggest heart! That has never changed. Know your own worth, and remember when people don't take the time to invest in you... You might want to re-evaluate that relationship?

I have learned a valuable lesson that only God can teach you. For the longest time I have been sowing into people and things, and **NEVER GAINED A THING**, so I thought. People are people, some know and others don't, but I learned so much. I am natural **GIVER**! I was able to develop my gifting, and skill to propel me to where I am now and where I am going.

It never once crossed my mind to be looking for the pats on the back or a mere thank you, but every once in a while it is nice to know that you're appreciated. I just wanted to be a blessing to people in general. People from all walks of life, people that follow Christ are always thinking that what I do is for **FREE**! I have had to tell them... What gave you that idea? Really? I have expenses too... the most importantly my **TIME**! I have **PAID THE PRICE TO WALK IN THESE SHOES!**

For so long I always wanted to be useful, and to not feel like I was some waste of space that I'd been made to feel like. I don't leave in that place anymore... Thank you Jesus!

I did spend my fair share of time in the secular school systems, and learned even more, but this is the deal breaker. What I got in these schools, I already knew... these schools and what they where teaching me now, are like 10 to 15 years behind, where I am. Don't get me wrong...

I am very grateful for the education. I have no idea at this point in my journey where the Lord and I will go, but wherever He decides, I am sure I will be equipped for the task. It's like sometimes I already know what to do... when the situation, task, or job is presented. I would say, it's the wisdom of God, I so rely on Holy Spirit and not man... In general I have learned that keeping God first... and truly has been my hope for a better outcome.

Man Down!

We live in a world where sororities and fraternities are building up
those UnGodly things
And false truths within many of our local churches
From Greek signage, cat calls, chants and stomp the yards in your
pulpits
All in your bling, bling,
The so call finer things that money brings
Meaning tithes and offerings
Can buy
But why ask why?

To the So You Think You Can Preach reality television shows?
Sleep around with another man's wife; let the truth be told,
Get boo'd up with some random dude,
Because he's fine as the aged old wine,
Your lustful tastiness of sinful treats,
But you still think that you worship me?
Down to your flagging of colors and Greek clothing,
RUSH party week, of drunkenness and lewd after hours activities
To look down your nose of the next, which is your brother?

You Allpha and OhMega and he's Sigma Baita
Or whatever he wants to be?
I see you and I AM not pleased
By that of which I see
I AM ALL SEEING and ALL KNOWING,
But you pretend that you are near Me,
But I turn My head and ear because of your filthy scent
And it is cold as the dead of winter

Need I mind you, that you've turned your heart back to stone
And your love away from Me,
To whore after the unrighteous and ungodly things
Did I not come to set the captives free?
I speak against the powers of darkness that lies beneath

Ornitha Danielle

In your cults of familiarities,
Of over religiousness and traditional realities,
relying by your own powers vested in you
Your secret hand shakes, private meetings, and church conventions
that don't even include Me.
How can this be?

For I died on a cross publicly
For ALL to see
That it was Me that chose you, not that you chose Me.
I gave MY LIFE FOR ALL HUMANITY!
Be set apart for my work only,
But you've given continuous work and employment security
to the enemy and the darkness that be.

You preach of a world that is not from here,
But do you believe what you speak
Oh My children learn to practice what you preach.

Stand not behind your Greek shows that mask itself
in public and say that it's for the betterment of this community,
When in the next sentence you are filled with rage and envy

Pimps in suits learning how to go by the book of diabolical systems
Running games and playing in the races of
This political agenda machine
illegal contracts, no integrity, or humility
doing business and calling it Me
God rewards those who wait? What?
The blessing of the LORD makes a person rich, and he adds no
sorrow with it

The way that things should be is; loving my Son first
Who freed your from Adam's and Eve's curse
Laying down your ways of ungodliness
To enjoy life in its fullness

Come my child, my chosen one, to be set apart

All just for Me
There's a greater place that you will dwell
With Me for All entirety
I have prepare a place for you in the presence of the enemy
There's no room at this table
Need I remind you of the story when Cain rose up against Able
There's been so much blood shed across the
land; that was never apart of My Plan

Your cup shall run of over
Be Holy for I AM Holy
Jesus Christ is the only way
So, please make up your mind today

For He is the truth and the light
To set you free
Remember the day of brutality
His skin was ripped from the bones
He bled and called you His own
Nails driven into His flesh
A crown of throne that was placed on His head
So now you are My Bride that I do wed

Hurt Issues Are A Heart Issue?

If I had a dollar for every disappointment, discouragement, and every shattered dream I would be miserable and wealthy individual. Many have said a many thing about, the dreams and ambitions in life that I have set for myself, but I am doing what I love to do at the end of the day. There's no greater pleasure than to walk in the things that God placed in you. I rather leave this earth knowing that by what I exemplified in my life, and how I was *ALWAYS* of service to others.

Sometimes when I think back over my journey, a many doors closed in my face, and many no's, where not interested, or you're just too over qualified for this type of work, do you mind working for nothing?

When I am given the opportunity to speak to other women and young ladies one thing that I make sure that I tell them. It always matters to God, and that He loves you very much, in spite of what you will ever do or don't do. Healing begins to take place on the outside… the reason I say that, is this just like a sore, it gets a scab… the scab is to protect that tender place underneath, however, once that scab is peeled or rubbed off, the inside is exposed, to elements, and sometimes it will start to bleed… why?

Because underneath hasn't or didn't have what it needed to heal. Sometimes, people will try to make you feel in less than the person that God called you to be, but you have to find the solace in knowing that without a doubt that God is your **VINDICATOR** and will get the **GLORY** in the **END**!

As, I am writing my heart couldn't help for the many places that I have walked where I've allowed the feelings of others to cause me to not move as Holy Spirit would have me to move. To be totally honest, things that people can say, can take root down in your core, but we have Jesus that will come in and remove it, if we only would allow Him too. I have never been the one to want to open up about some of the many things that I've had to walk through.

Depression is real and very serious if it's not treated, but we as believers have to be very mindful that we don't re-injury God's people. Hurt issues are a real heart issue in fact. But because of the love of one (Christ), and Him coming to rescue us from these traps of enemy that would want to make us feel less than we are. Some things do take a great deal of time, a process to get over, another process to heal and another process to move forward. Will there ever be a point in time to be healed from heart issues?

YES! As, I said before it does take time to mend… but only God can mend a broken vessel the heart of man. We try to repair it, but guess what it's only temporary a sense of falseness of getting over it, when God does it shall remain mended.

Truth of the matter is this. We can spend a great deal of time trying to get the healing instead of allowing the things to bring us to a place to be healed. I for one have spent so much time trying to fix things that are broken, only to realize that I needed God to fix it and to heal me in the process. With man it's only for a while, but with God its **FOREVER**. Even in this place of coming face to face with some things in our lives, it brings on a greater deliverance that is needed.

There's this old saying, you can lead a horse to water, but you can't make it drink from it. I believe that many of us pretend that we've come to this place, of being healed, but when we're truly **SEEKING GOD AND PRAYING**, that we begin to **SEE THE EVEN BIGGER PICTURE**. That picture would be Jesus Christ, one that **WAS** perfect in everything, as well as in the eyes of His father, was blameless, and yet He became sin for a US that we would have everlasting life. So even our daily issues, hang-ups, struggles or mistakes, we should love God more than what we see, in my own opinion these are smokescreens that the enemy tends to bring us, to cause to go to the right or the left, instead of keeping our eyes on **HIM (GOD)**. So today, I ask you whatever you're facing will you or are you willing to do what it takes to become freed of this, which isn't the will of God for your life.

First Responder?

You know years ago, I set out to be a First Responder! I wanted to be a Paramedic and later advance to Flight Nurse. During my internship riding with Memphis Fire and Police for 2-days. Which would be 2 twelve hours shifts. That is no easy job or task. I had considered the task, the job and dangers that I would face everyday. I had accepted the risk...

The ultimate job for me at the time was this, my husband wasn't the least bit happy about this line of work, but he's ALWAYS SUPPORTED ME! I was really great at it! During my ride... I SAW SO MUCH! Within the first 3 hours of my day... I think I had been to several car accidents with a scared child, a person on street meds looking for their next fix, to a possible heartache.

Why am I sharing this... well one I think sometimes we can lose sight of those that are in these jobs, and have chosen this profession as career. They do get tired, they are overworked and underpaid, and sometimes they do come in contact with more criminals than we care to mention. I'm not changing my position on what's been happening around us, but we have to look at what the real problem is...

Now.... during my training and study... before an EMT or Paramedic can even have access to the scene... we have to wait for Police and Fire Dept. to secure it, for our safety. Then sometimes the ones that are there to protect you while on the job, you are now treating them from the crowd, that has gotten out of hand, for different reasons could be from robberies, car accidents, fires, GS, to sick people in the home.

Mind you, that when you are called to come to a scene, you are running off pure adrenaline, and once everything is over, you literally CRASH! There's a lot of debriefing that has to take place you the mind of those that are there. I will never forget my job as a Emergency Dispatcher... to be the First Responder via phone...

You hear so much and sometimes can actually see what taking place is; well it was that way for me. There's never enough money in a day that could bring a person back home that lost their life in the line of duty. Day after day...

I have tried to make sense of the many stressors of our own lives... We as a people can do much more than we think... It does start at home.... we have to teach our children how to respect others, and that it is okay to have a differences of opinion.

The Blossoming Rose

The petals have started to open
Yet in still the sweet scent that glides in the air
Often reminds us of the world we do share
Needless to say, that one day God will come again just wait and see
It is all for **HIS** Glory
I am reminded of the stories that told of His journey
At the twinkling of an eye,
We will see Him soon

I can't help but think that as I read about what He went through,
Intellectually we haven't fully dismiss that part
That all He did was from his broken heart...

Loving what he created, and we went in the other directions
Longing for us to love Him back,
He chased us and did everything to get our attention
He was beaten, mistreated and crucified
That somehow we'd see
Him for the Savior that He is

Your Light Should Not Be Hidden

I have been most silent here for these days... one is because there's been this need to even more vocal with God, you may wonder how much more vocal can you be? Blessing the name of the Lord! With everything that is going on all around and in us that sometimes we tend to lose sight of what is very important to God.

We forget our direction; we forget the sight of our dreams, our **FIRST LOVE**! Remember John 15:16. You did not choose me, but I chose you and appointed you so that you might go and bear fruit-- fruit that will last--and so that whatever you ask in my name the Father will give you.

I am so convinced that you can throw people a lifeline and because of their hearts they will miss it every single time. I can say I myself have been on the other end needing to be rescued a many times in my own life. Here I am just listening to the many trials and tribulations others go through... God your people are so oppressed and myself included... I know that I am not of this world.

I refuse to believe that this is the way things will end. When we spend less time pointing finger and cursing one another and more time praying uplifting one another and then we can see the **LIGHT** at the other end of the tunnel. That we really need a savior!

That we really need **JESUS** more **NOW**! Why? 2 Chronicles 7:14if my people, who are called by my name, will humble themselves and pray and seek my face and turn from their wicked ways, then I will hear from heaven, and I will forgive their sin and will heal their land.

Wounds Healed

We need to pray for our cities and the people in them, from those that make decisions on our behalf! We are loosing too many souls due to these random acts of violence! Spend less time trying to diagnose a situation and more time in the presence of God to lift up those who are unable to pray for themselves. Just like someone somewhere prayed for you...

If you know anything about the hard thing, a walk that sometimes you have to face it alone... and that road can be difficult, it's a process that we try to get ahead of that to jump to the finish line?

Now, I am going to say... as I have been studying, and seeing the authority in which many in the bible walked and lived by demonstration... how come we can't exercise that same authority? (Do we see these as just stories?) Stop finger pointing and start kneeling... too much being placed in the spirit... we are aware that the enemy is behind these acts... I know that God's spirit is greater than that of any devil!

People are in need of much healing and deliverance for various reasons... neither of us are obsolete when it comes to warfare... No one is perfect, but we are striving for perfection with God's help, and strength. Too much of this and less of that... Put your lips to pray! Operate in your sphere of authority people of God!

Use wisdom, and learn how to war in the spirit instead of in the natural... It's sad to know that we've become a people of accusations, ideals, and could've and what should have happened, or didn't anyone see or know that this was going on? The God that I serve reveals things to those that seek to know... which gives you access to pray into a situation.

A Community That Needs Healing

I don't know what more heartbreaking at times with everything going on in the world, crimes against children, elderly, the homeless, to the talks of racism on all sides... and what I mean by that is... lighter skin African women is to be more desirable for the face of things. Or all African American men are deadbeats, pimps and love wearing their pants tight or falling down under the behinds?

As well as other races are faced with the stereotypes... either they're on crystal meth, or someone has ties to the **KKK**. I mean I could keep going... then there's the crimes we commit against each other. Let's not get it twisted okay. I'm not talking about coming in agreement with people who are in their sinful acts, but seem to want down play it, to a lesser charge? Excuse me, but where do they do that at?

The state of the church... I will say this. It's beyond getting the acts together! Can I really, explain this? Too many of us know the linguistics of "quote on quote" "how to do" verses "how to be" the church. See we have much work to do... then to be worried about the less meaningless things... like having zoning issues for park in a neighborhood where there's nowhere safe for a child play anymore, with thoughts of a toddler being hit by a stray bullet...

These are things that should be tipping the bowl in heaven over! The injustice for all mankind... when it comes to us saying we believe in God, and that we follow Christ Jesus, but we there's a bit of prejudice in the heart of man. Often times people are so quick to run to trash, negativity, but get up Sunday morning and bless God, but in the parking lot and won't even speak to a fellow labor? Why? Here's why?

It's because they got the parking spot you always park in all the time. So you don't speak. Better yet many people have left the building for various reasons; not because they don't love God, but have you ever took the time to ask the Lord why?

53

I was listening to something tonight, where God pulled people out of places to mend, and clean them up due to soulish desires, abuse, shame, dying this list could go on. It does take God to yank people from themselves, but unfortunately they learn the hard way.

What does it matter if you go to church meaning outfit on fleek, shoe cam ready, hair slayed, nails did... or you just got chopped up, or your gear is tight and ready to go hear some good preaching. But your fellow church member lights are about to get cut off. Or has anyone visit Mother that has been in the hospital because they couldn't afford their meds this month? I do get like this at times, because I just get so grieved when people saying God said, and I know what the Lord has told me.

I'm just saying well... if that where the case then why are we having this conversation? You may not have gotten the message, bells, don't work, red flags waving, several people have come to you, and here we are? Look I have been there, but quickly to repent, humble myself, accept the rebuke, get up and start over going in the opposite direction from the distraction.

That distraction if you're not careful could lead to destruction! www.repentance.com is for everyone! www.deliverance.org I'm not being funny I am very serious! Everything ain't God and everything ain't the devil either! Some of the problem is you! I remember growing up... there was this sheer fear of death that was in me, when it came to God.

See I grew up with the fear that God, was sitting on the throne ready to **STRIKE ME DOWN!** Nowadays there's no respect for God or each other. People will do and say anything and God is in it! Stop lying on God! God is **HOLY**! Check your real motives before God does! Smh... We gotta get it together!

Brokenness To Wholeness

Where I am at this point in my life, seriously it's only because of the blood of Christ Jesus! The constant chasing, because He loves me just that much! As I was working on my books as I am usually doing, where I am talking with Holy Spirit. I began to ask the Lord a question about my life, and where it is that He desires to take me, show me and guide me at this point.

What was revealed to me is this, that how much I mean to Him, and that it's very important that I stay in His will and on His path for my life. Then I saw the many times I missed it, and began to walk away from Him and how I broke His heart.

The Lord was allowing me to see, a lot of it was because of past hurt, rejection, and disappointment, much of it had to do with the expectations of others, and this mistreatment and that I trusted, and held in high regards. How can people love God and mistreat others, as bad as it was I became a human trashcan for others.

I was so turned off by "church" the physical building, not the people of God (***Let Me Say That***) church politics, churches 50 thousand programs, church elections, the walking on two sides of the fence where people had not only made God's word of none effect, but to disregard it as well. I myself have been a part of this foolishness as well, but thank God for Christ Jesus.

We can't continue to be one way before people and a different way behind closed doors. Let me say yes we all have character flaws, and difference of opinions. But there's **NO LOVE** because of it. We can agree to disagree doesn't make anyone less than what God created. God created you beautiful, and loves to sing over you; why are we placing the evil over people's lives?

Just because we see things different it doesn't make my opinion less important than that of someone else. What I have learned through my quiet time with God, developing a deep relationship with Him, I found peace and I've learned to love me!

If not loving myself isn't loving God and who created me; the very air that's in my lungs is because He made it possible! Indeed I loved God so much, but the demands of tradition and religion was sucking the very life out of me.

There was no abundant life in that, no love, no peace all I saw was death and rules that was too difficult to live in such a way, that praying for death was easier to envision. I'm sharing this why? Because in hopes of someone else becoming Free, Freedom is your too! Love is kind remember?

Let's really be about God's business, because sometimes, in having a bad day, which we all do, but your bad shouldn't be everyday... If you were generally nice it would show in everything that you do. Loving God truly in spirit is the only way we can do it and love His people the same way.

Walking In Purpose

I never thought in the many years that I have been alive that I would be where I am today. What I am saying is that with every mistake, decision, the ups and downs in life that I've had to stand in the midst of all of that and face the music! Some things where caused not of my own doing, but that which God was bringing me into...

Destiny and Purpose. As I stood, the **OIL** was flowing from within.

It has made me such a better person, not to take those situations for granted and learn from them, and help others, by sharing what God did for me in the midst of my life this far. I'm rejoicing even in my trials and tribulations. I have even learned how to become more humbled, having a Godly attitude, having **PATIENCE** in the midst.

It's one thing to live out your dreams, but another to hold fast to them, and not waiver in it. Finding you God, you will find your purpose.

Your Destiny Awaits

I was just sitting here working on a few things... I'm not sure if anyone ever experiences this, but I was just thinking to myself about how so many times we're every so quick to dismiss sin, for the sakes of pleasure...

That could be a number of things, whether it be food, shopping, and the other things that we tend to make excuses about or secretly partake in. Yes, I do understand that we "all" fall short, but what about the verses before that part and those after that...

I'm not judging but I'm wondering why certain things are okay, but others are not. Depending on the situation... I don't get that. I can be honest with myself... prior to my understanding, and doing what I knew was right or at least felt was right. Here's my testimony...

A few years ago, I was working on my first novel... I too know right from wrong, but because of my own desires, or fleshy mindset... I allowed that and what the enemy was trying to do, pervert the gifting that God placed in me...

I thought it was okay, since I was grown, and I was free to do, say and write whatever I wanted. Hey, who was I kidding its just a book right? Well sadly God wasn't having it. I tossed and turned for months regarding the nature of the book. How could I as a believer write something like that... when I say it was the opposite of Holy?

Loving The Beautiful Soul Within

It's something when God does a thing. To sit in awe of what an amazing opportunity to serve and worship **HIM**! I can remember times before when I thought that I had it **ALL** together, but only realized that I was in need of **HIM**.

 I never acted arrogant or snobbish toward others nothing like. I just wanted to do my thing, I felt like I wasn't harming anyone, so I thought. I was the very one being harmed by doing the opposite of what God had said, being disobedient, **BUT THANK GOD FOR GRACE**! We will talk about God's Grace, later. That will truly bless you!

Freedom in Christ is truly the most **BE-YOU-TIFUL** thing **EVER**! I've walked into a new season of things and yet to come. As I soar to greater realms of God, and breaking of what if's, should haves, and could haves. God's will and plans for my life.

In the book of Jeremiah 29:11! Do I need to say more? I think I will pause right there. I have learned to use the very things that God placed in me, and not to look down on what God's given, because others' didn't like it or thought it wasn't important enough. God placed unique gifts in us to be a blessing to others, even ourselves. Be kind to one another, and be sure to be a blessing and not burden.

Dream A Dream … A Poetic Dream...

I couldn't help but remember the picture that was presented right
before my eyes to see, a picture of people talking, walking and about
so casually, it seemed like I watching a scene from a hit movie
"Quiet on the set is what I hear now
As I am writing these things down"

Two young ladies conversing back and forth,
Laughing among each other as if there was a joke.
One in a black and white blouse and with furry pink hat
The other in a black dress,
Surely she was dressed to impress
Must have been some dinner party by the way they there were
dressed,
And they seemed to have white coffee mugs in hands
As, they were leaving out of the kitchen to entertain their guest

I looked a little closer to see more, as the vision was so clear, even
with my eyes closed shut
I tried to awake, but there was so much more to see
So I couldn't wait
Because this dream had a date with me
And I with it,
So let me speed up the pace a bit

The more I looked the excitement grew,
Then there was this man standing there in a
Red three-piece suit,
He never spoke,
He just walked around and took notes
And from the looks of it
He was clearly no joke

I tried to awaken once again,
But I looked to my left and
There was this pen, one that I had not seen before,

But just next to it was this White door,
Partly opened now it piqued my interest,
But wait that's not even the best part
However, there's more to this mystery that I am witnessing,
Trying wake-up from this that I see,
It has totally overwhelmed me

As, I could hear the things all around and about me you see,
My phone buzzing with notification, crazily.
I asked God was I really sleep already?
He said to me,
"Remember all that you see"

I moved a little closer
I see more people even some that I knew
And others I had no clue of who they are,
But in my mind, it was so much to behold,

There's so much about this story
That has yet to be told
With my thoughts running wild,
I have to take some time to process all of this now

Then it shifted to this place with tons of building, sidewalks and
trees, I said to myself I remember these things, I had been here
before
I looked up at this lady on the second floor, she hurried away, as I
waved and tried to get her attention,
I know who she is but she was hiding
Now what gives?
Her physical body was a bit strange,
With this distended abdomen, on that would be tiny frame
It wasn't a pregnancy you see,
It was something that was taking life within this being.
I stood there surveying the scenery once more,
Making mental notes and eating a bitter piece of dark chocolate
Candy,
Then I turned around, for some reason;

There I was in a car still looking, but out of the window,
Of what was before me

The car never moved
I just sat there like
I was watching the evening news
Then I grew tired, but I was still in this dream,
That I am trying to awake from immediately
Class is now in session, I'm sure there is a lesson to be learned, but
right now I don't see it, I am going to fail this mid-term

I arrive to this class and everyone is piled up in one room, sitting
and watching some special program on TV
It appeared to be some medical show that was on

I was still trying to wake up,
But the more I struggled to get up,
The deeper into this dream I went
I then noticed these strange things appearing like mosquito bites on
my underneath my skin?
I was like wait what is this?
Back in the car I went again, only to lie down and rest a bit,
then a woman that I know very well comes over to try and talk to
me,
but I wasn't interested in anything that she had to say after blowing
me off earlier that day
Actually, I was wishing that she go away, but she said to me,
"I am trying to talk to you"
She looked at my arm and noticed the strange thing looking like
mosquito bites underneath my skin too
To me it seemed to have spreaded from one arm to the next
The woman said, "Let's get you to the doctor so they can check this
out".
Honestly, I wasn't the least moved by her concern or her plea, as I
said before I just wanted her to leave
Just then the actual telephone rings, and then
I was released from this poetic dream!

A Remarkable Journey

In place where time and distance often do meet
Here's my question somewhere along
this life's greatest journey
I have overcome defeat, but that I can't take any Glory,
because God was with me
The loving embrace, hearts beating, and destined to conquer all
Leaving at a moments trace

Wondering if I could recapture time that seemed to have passed by
Surely a photograph of this experience is forever etched in my mind
I have been waiting for this chance to exhale,
by my tears I shed, God collects
I do know that with God on my side, all is well

Crying over spilled milk no more
Because I know that God has the greatest plans
for me and my life in store
I have been given the authority to bombard heavens doors

Fellow servants that stand in the council of God are his angelic
messengers
Should I say, that I am yet discovering a newfound beauty in the
things around?
I am so waiting to see what God is about to do

As, I am writing I can't help but to think,
This message is written for all to receive the greatest gift is the one
that sent me
His name is Jesus, This story shall be told

Identity Revealed Through Intimacy

From a place of Brokenness to wholeness...

Knowing that God cares so much for me at one time I felt that I was so unworthy of love from anyone, especially from God. I've always felt that I had to be the perfect person, do everything right, go to church every Sunday, and Sunday school, bible study, pay my tithes, attend prayer meetings, revival, sing in the choir, I was taught how to do.

The power of journaling has been a lifeline to me.... Even to this day, I am still on the road to recovery day by day. I'm neither perfect, but I am being redefined. It takes time to allow God to do what needs to be done in your life, but you have to let him.

Once Upon A Time

I spent pretty much my entire life recording stuff. I keep a record of everything from wrapping papers of candy bars, to school programs, and magazine clippings. I have this photographic memory, of Total Recall Yes.

So I could remember stuff from weeks and maybe even years. Never knew that I was a scribe. It's funny you know, because now I've been freed and can truly live, walk, and enjoy the beauty of what Father has created in me.

I'm not all over the place, I am right where God wants me. Although I can do a number of things, I've learned to not limit God... or place myself in a box, which too can limit Him ability to move as He desire.

Greater Expectancy

When you are given clear instructions to go into a certain direction in life, nobody was there with you in the private time with the Lord, when He spoke... **ALWAYS** listen to God. If you move away from that plan or path that was shown you, chaos can enter into your midst, **DISTRACTIONS** or you will get off focus and out of alignment to what God has for your life.

Sometimes situations are stumbling blocks that would cause you to step out of character, or hinder the move of God, only out of frustration, but I want to encourage you today.... Move forward according to the plans of God, yes your plans do matter, just make sure that you seek God.

It's very important to be **OBEDIENT** to the call and the anointing that has been placed upon your life. Either you can move too fast, and miss it or you can move too slow and miss it. Learn to know the voice of God for yourself, from your own voice, and **STOP TALKING SOOOOO MUCH** to **OTHERS**, that have no clear direction or can't hear and trust God for themselves.

Learn how to pray and seek God until HIS peace comes. I will say this, there has been a many times when I know that God has told me to move, and run for my life and I did just that! If I hadn't done it, I would not be writing this message today. It's time to stop allowing others to pull from you, without being poured back into, its time to be replenished.

If you can trust God for your life, then you can trust him to take care of **YOU**, and those things that concern you as well. God wants us to prosper as our soul prospers. It's time to move into a new season of **EXPECTANCY!!!** To do **GREATER THINGS FOR THE KINGDOM OF GOD!!!**

Use The Master's Keys

Divinely Speaking: The word of the Lord we peculiar people of God have to **STOP** coming into agreement with the things of world. It is time to stop doing church as usual, that's old; God is bringing forth a new and fresh sound, new wine skins!

No more repeating someone else's messages. I Am doing, A new thing, a new thing, a new thing! Get ready for the Apostolic Prophetic thrusting like never before seen, and heard before, a new thing.

I Am sending many of you out as undercover agents to help free my people in this hour, from the traps, tricks, plans, plots and scheme of the enemy. I'm with you always. Write what you see and hear. You must record it! It's very important to write it down. Stand firm on my promises.

Expect me said the Lord, I'm doing a new thing, except me to speak, except me to answer concerning my will for the nations! Many of you are battling physically, mentally, emotionally and spiritually in this hour, but don't back down, stay on your post!

Pray always! The greater the trial, the greater the oil! Stay on the wall watchmen! Except to see me in the midst! I have given you keys and access to what you need in this hour. Protect the territories that I have given you, pray for one another, and again pray without ceasing!

As, I was mediating and talking to God this is what the Lord said. Be blessed beloved precious daughters and sons of the King!

Signs Of True and Real Maturity

I know that this is something that is never talked about too much, but it should be, but for me I can see growth even in myself, when it comes to dealing with others and myself. It doesn't matter about age, but when you come to a place where you choose to die to your own ways of doing things, but always doing it the correct way according to the way God would have you to do it.

In the midst of my walking with God, I pray for Death! What I mean is that I die to the things that would have me acting and handling things out in my flesh. That doesn't bring him glory, and lead others to Him. We should all pray for **DEATH**, because that is where we come to know more of **HIM**! Intimacy with the Lord is paramount, and there's no other way for me!

We can at times feel that we're correct, but when we are tapped in and **SOLD OUT** for God we can expect Him to pull those things up out of us, and make us handle those things. One thing is for sure... Prayer does change things, but it changes the one that is praying.

That's not so easy to do when you always wanna have the last word, or do whatever one feels in their mind or sight to be correct. The bible tells us to lean not to our own understanding...

Proverbs 21: 2-4 A person may think their own ways are right, but the **LORD** weighs the heart. The **LORD** is more pleased when we do what is right and just than when we offer him sacrifices. Haughty eyes, a proud heart, and evil actions are all sin. See what I mean? I don't know about anyone else, but when Holy Spirit puts you on check mode, you have no other choice, but to get it right. It causes us to deal with whatever issues that keeps coming up. Once that can be done, then true humility and maturity comes forth.

Grandma You Are Loved

You touch our very hearts right from the start
A grandma's love that could only come from Heaven above
From the beginning of this foundation
Of God's beautiful earth's creation

Even though we are apart now, Grandma we realize it's only for a
little while
God has called your name and said,
"Come on home and rest my child"
Many seasons may come and seasons may go
We'll remember the many stories that you often told

Deep inside we know you wanted to stay
We're missing you deeply each and everyday
There's no more suffering, no more heartache and no more pain
We're thankful that its peace you've made

Heavenly paradise is where you truly belong
Resting safely and securely in the Master's Arms
You're now walking the streets paved with gold
We're imaging you're shining brightly in your white robe

Upon your head is a beautiful crown adorned with many jewels
Remembering all the fun times that we've all had with you
We love and miss you and now that's the honest truth
There's not another Grandma that was quite like you

You are in the presence of the King
Where there is peace, liberty, and healing in his wings,
Grandma dance with your Heavenly Father as He takes the lead
In your new body, free from ALL pain and misery
You are home now and God has gotten the GLORY!

As HE has finished the ending to your beautiful life's story
The things we will keep in our hearts forever are memories

Ornitha Danielle

The legacy and treasures you left behind
Their all truly one of a kind

We can't believe how much time really does fly
Only God knows of our time from day to day,
Trust in Him Christ is the only way
There are no more hills and mountains for you to climb

Never did think we think we'll be standing here to saying goodbye
We are going to really miss you Grandma, as our souls and hearts
cry

Hope that we'd had just a little bit more time
We'd wished we knew, when we'll see you again
To enjoy your love and we could get just one last hug
Grandma we just thought we'd say that you will be missed and you
are
Truly Loved

Waiting Patiently Wednesday...The Wisdom of God!

What happens when all else fades? You should trust God.... during the course of our day; we can get so overwhelmed with the cares of this world. The bible tells us to cast our cares on Him, because He cares for us... 1st Peter 5:7 *Casting all your care upon him; for he careth for you.* I know that it can get hard at times when you are facing so many adversities when they are coming from all directions.

Isaiah 59:19 *so shall they fear the name of the Lord from the west, and his glory from the rising of the sun. When the enemy shall come in like a flood, the Spirit of the Lord shall lift up a standard against him.* I too have to remember that myself... I am human.

You've been equipped for a mighty work... Many of us don't always know in which direction that we are going because I do believe our assignments can change at any giving moment, without the need preparation.

Loving God with your whole heart.... Mark 12:*30 and thou shalt love the Lord thy God with all thy heart, and with all thy soul, and with all thy mind, and with all thy strength: this is the first commandment.* Believe it or not... our trials and tribulations aren't to destroy us, but to make us better, to teach us humility in our everyday walk.

Sometimes these things can cause us much discomfort? I have found that God is trying to bring us up in your thinking... Spirit-filled believers are to have the mind of Christ! 1st Corinthians 2:16 *for who hath known the mind of the Lord, that he may instruct him? But we have the mind of Christ.*

Have you been in this place of or find ourselves asking God why? I know I have been in that place to asking why? Then I am sure that we've all been told, we don't or are not suppose to question God? All my life, I've questioned God, not coming from a place of arrogance, but from a place of understanding.

Ornitha Danielle

Like many of you are still waiting for answers to those questions...
trust and believe that if we keep our eyes and ears open we will get
those needed answers. I know some will come immediately, and
others will take time to be answered.

But Seeing Through the Eyes of Christ

There are so many things that I could do, but I am having a little moment, all in my feelings... I decided to have a little down time today, watched a few movies, and I have been reminded of the things I use to dream about, and thought about as child... and to actually be living out loud in many of them.

All I ever wanted in my life was to be heard... I can remember when I was school; all I did was write... I lived in creativity; it was a very safe place for me.

Nothing else made any sense to me at all. I think my life took a turn by the time I was in 6th grade... I had to write a book report for English, but I think back then it was called Language Arts. Times have truly changed... There was never a moment that I didn't have a notepad, pen or pencil with, oh not to mention a book. My journey started very early, I became an avid reader... I read ***EVERYTHING***!

If there were words I read it... I also keep a diary... the cute ones with the keys, but I wrote so much that I had to switch to a journal, then from there it spiral notebooks... I think that so many times, we struggle to find ourselves, or be defined by the things that we do, or have achieved, there all fine, but there's so much more. I think I spent most of the time, being told what I could not do, or have, or whether my ideas where good or not.

That's no place for anyone to live... Then the unthinkable happened.... the very thing that I found comfort in was stripped... My diary/ journal was discovered.... when I about between 12 and 14, and from there I never wrote again! I didn't start writing again until I was about 18 or so... I had moved out on my own.

I've done my very best at the end of the day, living the best life that I can possibly live, and treating God's people with Love and respect, regardless of where they are in their walk with the Lord. Some maybe a little stronger than others, but the fact is this....

Am I exemplifying the Love God in what I do? Lord, keep me in place of humility, love and have compassion for your people. Father, forgive me where I have failed to do so, whether it was unknown to me, that I missed it.

I want to be pleasing to you, I want to represent you, I was sent here, by you to do a great work. For every soul that I will encounter, that I don't miss the opportunity to share your love.... Show me your Glory; heal me with your word.

Prayer is very essential and its God's will for us to live a life in this way... Pray without ceasing. When we fail to follow this we become weak, and at times can be bait for the tricks, plots and plans that the enemy have to throw along the path. If we would just simply give THANKS and Pray, we can begin to see the things in and around us change.

From a first hand account of what that looks like, although seeing things with the natural eye, would cause anyone to become alarmed, worried, frustrated, **BUT SEEING THROUGH THE EYES OF CHRIST!!**

That spiritual eye and having the understanding that **HIS PLANS**, are for Good and not evil that is over in the book of Jeremiah 29:11... I'm thankful that I grew up with a fear of God, I longed to understand and to become more and more like The Father in Heaven that created me for a time such as NOW!

When I learned to stop compromising, justifying and competing with the world, my vision began to change. No longer walking in the scope of Tunnel Vision, but having a new vision, one that is better than 20/20, seeing as God sees gives me hope, and not an illusion as the world would refer to it.

Let's not put the PRO in Procrastination. This problem can lead to other problems, whether its in business, school or hobbies. If we want to be taken serious in what we do, we have to learn how to have that follow through type of mindset. Finish what you start!

Never take on more if you're not completing what you already have. Zeal can have us starting off to a great start; the thrill of excitability, and once that comes down, that along with the other things end up incomplete. Revisit those things again... Don't be robbed of your ability, by the inability to move past ***PROcrastination***. Put a stop to it, your future is depending on it.

Transparency Moment

I'm crying tears of JOY, and sometimes that isn't always easy to do. This Butterfly Has Come Out of The Cocoon, and is now able to spread my beautiful wings and SOAR! I have been a bit quiet here in my sharing, BUT this journey of writing this book "God's Butterfly" Redefined for Purpose has by far been one of the toughest one to write so far, I have had to walk away and cried about a few things, now I am seeing so much of where I was, to where I am going these days.

Honestly the things that God has done and is doing in my life has been a JOURNEY! I'm not perfect, but I loved perfectly by the God that sees me, I know that GOD has been working on this one right here (I can be a bit much). Selfish I am not, I do get in my feelings and shut down... still working on that, thank God for His patience and grace.

On Another Note... I have had to deal with disappointments, that has been a HUGE struggle for me, and expectations of other people was another one... it works my nerves for people to tell me things and not follow through!

I have walked around for years with this feeling for so long, and I never get excited about things, because I am like it's not going to happen or I am going to get let down again! I've had a problem with people NOT showing up ever for me! (REJECTION)

Why am I sharing this? Well, I had a moment, where I am like you know what, it's whatever, I don't have time for this, I'm going to do me! I started seeing a pattern in my attitude about when people say things and do the opposite of it. Yeah, I do wear my HEART on my sleeve, and I can be a crybaby at times. Sometimes it makes you feel like okay, so what do they want...

I have feelings and they do matter, maybe not to everyone else, but to me and God. I don't have it all together in everything and may never get it all, but I know I love God and that He LOVES ME!

I love what I do... Never really saw this in the way that I am seeing it now. For many years I have been behind the scenes doing different things.... I am an organizer of many things, I love putting things together and watching those things unfold. Sidebar... I have always been a planner...

I have even been consulted on a few projects as well when it comes planning events, parties, weddings and etc. I had the liberty to work with a few dance and cheerleading teams, and been on a few many in my youth. Also, put my hands in designing the outfits for these teams as well.

Sometimes you never really see the beauty inside yourself, you downplay it most of the time. Just because I love God, and follow Him, doesn't mean that I have to stop living, and enjoying whom He created me to be from head to toe. I want to encourage you as you are reading the very words from this book. Be everything that God has written about you in the books.

Having a choice to create a new chapter in your life. Start letting go of people that seem to want to live in a place of drama. Writing a book, or a poem just to release those things unto the Lord, or just for you.

Waiting, waiting and waiting for the right time, making the time to do it is what is important to this process. We all find time to do everything else, but this is where it's time to go into your cocoon, and be revived of those old things.

Growing Pains

We've all come to that place in our daily walk with Jesus... that those growing pains are just that (growing pains). When there's a place to come higher in the things of God, we tend to allow fear, frustrations, past hurt, intimidation, rejection, or the ideas of others and condemnation to keep us or put us in bondage.

Those things aren't displaying the mind of Christ! In the scripture of 1st Corinthians 2:16 *for who hath known the mind of the Lord, that he may instruct him? But we have the mind of Christ. 1 John 4:4 ye are of God, little children, and have overcome them: because greater is he that is in you, than he that is in the world.*

Deciding on whether or not to receive all that God has for you is still a place where we are learning to let go, and walk in faith! As we are about to prepare for the deeper relation with Father, we should deeper look at ourselves; spend some much-needed alone time with our word, fasting, (however God leads you in this area) and praying.

Let me say I am no way near perfect, but I try to emulate Christ, most importantly, I love people and try to help in any way that I can. Something I will get, and others I will continue to walk out every day as any other believer on this side of heaven.

Not the Church as Usual

Something to think about what I consider church dynamics, not looking for a fight, just my observation, over the years. I am so thankful to be freed from a "building". I love God for being a **"REAL"** revealer of truth. You know that moment when everyone around you screams, but you are standing there scratching your head, yeah, but you know you missed it.

When your eyes and ears are opened. Going to church to learn how to become better people, to learn the word of God, and to be better in home, work, and in the community.

Along the way becoming experts at being petty, learning of God's word is only surface, got the rules and regulations down to the T, always in search for a word from the Lord, but refuse to eat it, can dance and shout, and can dress in the finest things Sunday, after Sunday, but **NO LOVE, NO COMPASSION** for those that are really dealing with some life and death situations. Can't pray, visiting other "buildings" for revival 5 times out of the year and year after year, good at traditional things and religious mindsets.

Have you ever thought to question is this the life that our God of **LOVE** speaks about or is this one of those things that has been taught for years upon years.

Having spiritual goals for yourself, studying out things that will give you greater insight into your specific calling. Seeing humanity strengthen for the greater, seeing lives restored, wholeness from a place of brokenness.

Getting tired of seeing people leaving these church "buildings" more broken than before, no better than before and been there over10 years. Still singing the same defeated songs, still saying the same ole' prayer, everything is still the same, same people leading in prayer and reading the same scriptures.

Sometimes you just have to ask yourself sometimes about what's going on with the picture? God does have much greater for you... Trust Him enough with your life; you can't afford to die in these unsuitable conditions, because too many people are looking for you, your ministry the one God placed in your belly.

It's just that simple... you don't have to wait 10 years to move in it. Move with God and know that many lives will be forever changed. Not the church as usual.

My Soapbox For the Day!!

It's always somewhat interesting when people that don't understand the basic principles of the Power of God and His Love in the life of a believer. To have a place where you can be forgiven of past sins, past faults, and past issues that are called "Life" in general.

When God can forgive us, why is it that "people" want to make your re-live those brief mishaps of your life, as if they are "PERFECT", that is the biggest lie ever told.

Now as a firm believer in Jesus Christ, in what He did, what He taught and how He showed us that it can be done. I think that it's okay to agree to disagree... The best way to settle that is to allow God's perfect will to be finished in His children.

If we take a look at everyone's life including our own, I'm sure we'd find something that we believe isn't correct in our own eyes...(Own Eyes). Now sin is sin... there's no way around that.

Somewhere throughout the day, sin is subject to creep in! Thank God for His grace! Thank God for laying down His life that I might live.

Fond Memory

It's not every day that you get to share your heart with people, but with what you do and having the right intentions. When it comes to my craft, I do take that with seriousness, I don't worship the gifting, but I do work at perfecting it. I've never really considered myself a great writer, but I spent most of my life writing. That was my way of expressing myself without interruptions or being talked over. Yes, I kept a diary… Of course I started off which the typical Dear Diary!?

I will never forget when I was in the 6th grade, there were two times when my writings would come into question. One was a book report I had to write a report on a book of my choice... and writing as a form of punishment for the entire class... write-offs... copying the dictionary which was somewhat funny to me, until the teacher decided to read them.

Writing the dictionary was way too boring for me, so I began writing a story. Which had me sent to the office, and to talk to the guidance counselor and phone call home all because of these write-offs. That was too funny!! My imagination got the best of me.

I've always carried a notebook, pen and book everywhere I went. First scenario... I was a huge fan of those Wal-Mart books for $4.88 romance type of books. My mom would buy me those books when we went to the store... she's shopping and off I go to the book section.

I got this book and honestly, for the life of me, I can't understand why, but I read the back of the book to see if I actually wanted to read it. I think I had read the first chapter by now... so I had to have it! This book was based on three girlfriends... Friends forever, so I read this book in like 2 days! I really thing it was the cover and maybe too what I read also.

The friends names where Toni, Karen and Samantha who they called Sam…

Yes! I will kill a book when it read it! I had two weeks to write this book report. It took me the entire two weeks to write this report, balls of paper on the floor, in the trash and in the bed...and not to mention my brother Alex drooling on few sheets too, that caused me to have to start over again. I think he was like 6 or 8 months old, yeah now that I think about it, he even snatched my paper and pencil. Kid brothers right, you just have to love them.

Oh almost forgot.... the best book report would get a 1st place ribbon, book report placed outside the classroom door and ice cream for lunch. Hey, sounds good to me, now mind you, I never thought that anything that I would write would get noticed. The chances of it being read? I worked on that book report, until I was finally satisfied with what I has written.

There were only three six-grade classes at my school, and they were broken down into teams. Of course you had your straight A students your Average then your not so below average students. I wasn't a straight A student, by this time, but I did fairly well in school. English, Science, History, Spelling, and Writing I loved oh and Art/Music, Math not so much.

Oh let me tell you what happened with book report.... The English teacher was going to grade them, and judge all of the students. So, the best 3 or top 3, 1st, 2nd & 3rd place winners will be announced. My heart was pounding like crazy, because the book reports are due! I turned my book report in, I decorated my folder, I was really proud of it.

 I am not sure how long it was before the grades would comeback, which to me it seemed like forever! I think I had written maybe like one or two paragraphs. Thank goodness, we didn't have to type and double space... handwriting was the thing. I want to say it may have been a week or more when we got the grade?

I was just sitting there like there's no way that I would win anything let alone a writing contest. The English teacher's name was Mrs. Suggs… very jazzy lady, with these long fingernails. That afternoon, she started talking about, sentence structure, and how to write a good book report, then she said however one student did such a great job, but there could only be one 1st place winner, but I want to encourage everyone to keep writing, and in time writing book reports will be a piece of cake.

Then I heard her call my name!! Then she began reading my book report out loud in front of the entire class. By this point I was like Charlie Brown, you know the teacher that nobody ever knew what she was saying? I sat there, in a daze-thinking wait a minute did she say that I won!

Now, she said, "Overall of the 3 teams Danielle had the best book report!" Congratulations! Here's where it gets tricky. Danielle, can you bring the book that you read to school tomorrow, because I want to look at it? I was wondering why she wanted to see the book, then I heard one of the students say, bet she didn't even write her own book report, she might copied it from somewhere or had someone write it for her? That came from one of the straight A students.

Honestly, I didn't care… I was getting that ice cream for lunch!! That entire day… I got the strangest looks from the students, not my friends of course. I brought the book to school the next day, and she read the back to the book, and asked me if I had written this book report by myself? I looked at her, and said yes ma'am I did. I am not sure if she thought I was honest, but that caused me to question my writings every since, I was afraid to share my writings that it would be judged like that.

Prayer and Training are Essential to the Destination

Prayer is so very essential to our destination in life, not just the natural aspects, but clearly the spiritual dynamics. Without it we'll be navigating about aimless and fueling off of others information and never seeking God for clarity.

We can even consider a thing out of our own will. I've found this to be so true... one can't pilot an aircraft or car without the tools (education and actually training) to do so, we need fundamental tools and experience to do so. Although we can have the basics but we are not free of error, because we do miss it.

We can read tons of books on how to operate a plane, but it will not be of any use until we actually have to do it alone. That means sitting in the pilots' seat and looking at the dashboard. It's really something the things that we see and hear as Holy Spirit opens our eyes and ears to.

Remember the point of reference... over in the books of Acts in the 19th chapter the 15th verse. What I found so sharply profound was that as they (Some Jews were faced with a situation). They were not equipped for the assignment.... they tried to stand in place that they were never called to... to go head on with the enemy, and do you that.

You see our taskmasters know what we can handle and what we cannot for that matter. I know people love to think that they are equipped for a place, but we better make sure that it's God's leading, and not the enemy leading us into a place to have us overtaken by his partners in crimes. So one day this group of men decided to cast out a demon... but they had never encountered a spirit like the one on this particular day.

In verse 13, it states that they went around driving out evil spirits tried to invoke the name of the Lord over those that where oppressed by a demon, but this time this one fought back, and told them that those that they spoke of they knew, and asked who are you? And at that moment the enemy overtook them! We don't want to try and operate in a manner in which we've not been trained for.

Step of Faith into The Unknown Realms with God

One of the most difficult decisions that I had to make in my life was to take a step of faith into the unknown realm with God! I totally walked away for traditions of men, and what is the normalness and ideals of church dynamics. I always have a lot to say, but sometimes have the hardest of times putting it together until I put pen to paper, or finger to keyboard whichever comes first.

For those that may not know, which is no secret I am what many would call a (PK that means Preacher's Kid). I had to say that's not a label that I ever liked one bit. Anyway, I grew up in and around church, I seen a lot, heard a lot and experienced a lot, from denominations, who's not preaching this or that.

Until I sought the Lord on my own, when you get to a place where things around you aren't making sense, but everyone is saying one thing and doing the latter. This is not to place blame on anyone, it's my account of what I saw, heard and experienced at different times during my journey to knowing God now.

I've always been a believer of the WORD of God, not the Traditions and the Religious things of placing or keeping individuals in bondage. Then I began to in my own private time by penning... it was my alone time with the God. I didn't know that then or understand why, but I would ask God a lot of times why it was this way, or why did His people that loved him behaved in such manners.

When you decide to follow God, truly and fully, and to many people you may look as though you have lost your mind, or seem like you are all over the place. Coming to a place of full understanding of what God is doing in your own life. See what God is saying to you about your direction for your own life for that matter.

87

I've been in writing mode, working on a number of projects. And this occurred to me. Do you ever think that I would do anything to hurt you? I'm preparing you for what is to come next in destiny and purpose with me. So, me being me, I say well sometimes I don't see what you are doing Lord. I have to laugh at myself too sometimes.

There's one thing that I do know that God never leads us into a place without the proper training, sometimes you've already been equipped for what you're about to encounter. I can't help but think about David, as he was about to stand face to face with Goliath. Had he ever fought a giant before? He didn't think for a moment that He was unable to, but He knew that it was his appointed time to face the battle of life.

 David was surrounded by men that where equipped and trained to engage in physical warfare or battle with the enemy. This is the understanding that I have from studies, of David defeating Goliath. Sometimes to doesn't take a lot to defeat an enemy of God, or bring about a shifting of things when God has a plan for our lives that we never see, but only needs us to be willing for the change. I'm sure even David was ridicule for even attempting to do such a thing.

God will use the very tools that you have if you would allow Him to move in the ways that He wants. What could have been on David's mind at the time of him stepping up and out on faith into a new realm of the unknown with God?

 It was his willingness to please God nothing more or less than that. Remember David was a man after God's own heart! This wasn't something that happened when he was older, but happened in his youth, somewhere the lines as a teen.

I Am Poetry In Motion

I Am Poetry in Motion,
Sitting in the sun, with the wind pressing
Gently against my cheek
Listening to the baby blue birds' soft tweets
In tuned to the time and space around,
Glimpses of Heaven is so profound,
But the reality is that
I am poetry in motion

Vibrations, mores codes and mathematical equations
The synchronization of clocks,
But when it comes to the precise timing on the clock that has been
created by the Master's hand

Who makes the world go round?
Spinning on its axel,
The multitude of stars that dance with routines of twirls,
And gliding in the galaxy on high to infinity and beyond?
I am poetry in motion

Or could it be the orbiting of planets
That happens to be on an invisible string
That moves about as they please,
But somehow we are unable to comprehend the spiritual things
The body is composed of atoms, matter, a hint of Adam's ale,
protons, neutrons and cells;
I am poetry in motion

Air filled lungs, blood flowing throughout veins; it was designed at
the Master's delight, fitted and fashioned in His image.
Part Spiritual the other part natural; which can be seen…
I am poetry in motion

Bodies derived by billions of numbers, Ph. balances, blood
pressures, and not forgetting the heights and weight of everything,
these things stream continuously,
But each one is calculate differently
I am poetry in motion

I am the one specifically; unexplained being that only makes pure
sense to the Author
How many muscle does it take to smile or laugh
Is it genetics or could it be just the
Spirit of A Holy God
Coursing in me; I am unique,
I am the only like me; created for purpose and destiny
I am poetry in motion

The atmosphere in which we exist not in some black abyss
Jesus Christ was betrayed by a kiss
One that was deadly
In more ways than one
It was an expensive price to pay
On that faithful day
I am poetry in motion

Judas didn't really realize that magnitude of what he did
For several pieces of silver to give up Jesus Christ
Who then later paid that ultimate price?
We can try to forget of the scriptures we read
About the crown of thrones that was placed on His head

On a cross He gave up His life
Never thinking twice of the sacrifice He made
Because I was the one His father gave
I am poetry in motion

Jesus Loves Me

Jesus loves me this I know, not just because the bible tells me, but also because He told me so

Although I might be weak,

But He is strong,
Yes, Jesus loves me

He loves me, because He gave up His life for me, He paid the ultimate price for the crimes that I would commit

Oh yes, Jesus Love me... it had nothing to do with the skin that I am, meaning how dark my melanin is, nor about where I live, but knowing that He lives in me

Oh yes Jesus loves me... see I seek to please Him in everything that I do, I seek to walk by the example that He left behind

Oh yes, Jesus loves me, because He forgives me, His grace and mercy will follow me... new mercies are renewed daily

Oh yes, Jesus loves me and this

I DO KNOW!

What's Love Have To Do With It?

What does LOVE got to do with it? It HAS EVERYTHING TO DO WITH IT. *(Love Has **EVERYTHING** to do with it!!)*

Although we are NOT perfect, but I do believe that there are places in our daily lives that need work. I couldn't help but to tap into what Holy Spirit is saying to me earlier today. I'm sure that we can find things in our life that needs or has been under construction for sometime now.

I know am talking to myself here... I haven't been the best at LOVE, but as I have matured in my relationship with God the lover of my soul, even when the very things that I did at times didn't display that I was one of His, or that I even knew Him.

How can we say that we follow Him acting anything less than what He required? I'm can be just as serious at times, and can be silly at times too, but we should practice on how to love, and learn how to allow others to love you.

Ephesians 4:12-13 For the perfecting of the saints, for the work of the ministry, for the edifying of the body of Christ: Till we all come in the unity of the faith, and of the knowledge of the Son of God, unto a perfect man, unto the measure of the stature of the fullness of Christ:

Do You Remember?

Can you ever remember a time in your life when all you did was church? I'm a preachers' kid; which is lack of a better term of cliché. As, a child I can remember going to other churches for Choir day, Men's Day, Women's Day, Youth Day, Usher's Day Deacons, mothers and missionary Day & Pastor & Appreciation day.

I really liked most of them, but extremely terrified of most of the guest speakers or should I say MC. There was this one pastor that most of the kids tired to imitate after service each time I would try, I would end up with a headache and a sore throat.

Be wise of what is incubation within your ministries because there are people watching, we don't need more cloning and more mini ME's to act just like you!

Oh I almost forgot there was a few pastor's as a child that I was afraid of because of what I heard and saw was screaming and sweating and wiping the foreheads, but then I look around and everyone saying *"amening"*, take your time pastor, teach pastor or you preaching today". I know that people shouldn't encourage this behavior.

Not all the time but most of the time I would copy down the scriptures, this was in my youth. We as Kingdom Child walking around with Kingdom Citizenship, we to need display and should want to act accordingly. For with Christ living in us... and the having the mind of Christ.

What I am saying here go back and get a refresher course taught by Holy Spirit, and sit down in your alone time with Him... because what was one, is something different. We need to be watchmen on the walls? We new teaching, let this new generation something to hold onto.

Don't get me wrong about these services, but don't rebuke people because their whole lives in not in these services. Don't try to cause people to live in a place of bondage because the repeated yokes the man has placed around you.

Living With No Regrets

When life isn't picture perfect,
but you are thanking God for every single moment. Start living your
without regrets. Loving the imperfections of you. Looking deep in a
mirror you will find something that you wish to change... hair, skin,
weight, style and more.

The things that we can change... but what that mirror doesn't change
is our attitudes. How we see ourselves. What if we start looking
through the eyes of Jesus Christ we would see what He sees. I keep
hearing look through my eyes... Christ views are what matters most,
and learning to live in this life without regrets.

Until a person can embrace their pass, meaning how can you become
the woman or man and learn to walk in the shoes that you admire so
much. Sometimes you have to learn how to walk first before you can
run...The higher the hill the harder the fall. Experience!

My Pen

This one is my pen, although there maybe many like this one,
But this one is mine
Crafted to fit the hands of the author, who is one of a kind?
This pen is mine
My pen, which found its way to me, we tell of the many things that I
inscribe prophetically

My pen and I tell of dreams, histories, realties, and unspoken
prophecies

The ink can be an array of colors, but when it comes to Holy Spirit
there is no other
I am the blood-dipped letter of Jesus Christ
So my pen and I have so much in common I am the letter and it
creates letters

Black, red, blue, pink or green writing about the unforeseen
mysteries
Wars all around this world, and even in the heart of others,
Sometimes when writing I cry from the wells of my pen
My Pen
My Pen
My pen

What happened as I write?
Courses of things turn, because I have been unction to write with my
pen
My Pen and I have so much to say, we declare healings, victories,
and changes in foreign polices, even more you see

My pen and I pled the blood of Jesus Christ
His blood is pure untainted
My pen caress this paper
Hard as can be, the evidence of the impression bleeding through to
other pages

95

Infectious as it maybe I pray that you understand every word in what
I speak
My Pen
My Pen
My Pen

This Is My Roar

Can you hear me roar, from within
Its as strong as the wind
Listen closely for what I speak, my voice is no longer weak
I'm coming forth bold
What's in me has to be told

My vocal projection has amplified
But it is God that is glorified
It's been locked up for a long time
For this can't wait, I can prophesy

With this roaring on the inside
The natural man has been put aside
Holy Spirit do what you must do
I will forever worship you
Your word is true, I fear none,
Because you are God's ONLY begotten son
But before then there was none

You cared just that much for me
You died so I can be free
So excuse the vibration of this roar
Knocking down idol imagery to the floor

There can't be anything raising
Higher than the ONE that should be
One day He will come again for the world to see

With Holy Spirit inside of me watch the enemy of darkness flee
He runs away, because of this roar he cannot take,
It makes the ground shake
I roar louder to tell about the good news
The things that Christ went through,
And how he shed His blood for me and you
It's not some fairytale you see, Christ laid down His life for you and

me

His love is unconditional you see
He defeat the adversary
At the place called Calvary
So excuse me as I roar, I have too; don't you see
Heaven is listening!

Still People

I know that this is different: In order for you to grow, and spread your wing you have to let go, and move away from those things in around and about you. Why? Because it is **STILL**! As I began to search online conserving the very word STILL. It is an adjective and the word is describe as motionless, not moving a muscle, like a statue. Here are a few examples that I have come up with.

Stay away from still people:

Still haven't matured in the things of God
Still hanging on to the past
Still unable to move forward
Still complaining
Still bitter
Still petty
Still hating
Still walking in unforgiveness
Still bouncing from church to church
Still don't believe that they are in the same place that they were years ago
Still can't see that they are wrong in certain situations

Still unbelieving

Still refuse to apologize

Still feeling like someone owes us something

Still can't understand the way life is

Still not willing to accept correction

Still refuse to submit to authority

This list could go on forever! However, these are some of the ones that I believe that can hinder the greater things that God wants to take us to. When we realize that every one can't go with us. When we refuse to follow the order that has been set for us.

I'm sure we have found ourselves in many of theses situations; we are so still in some areas, that we can't experience the wonderful things of God. It's not God that fails us, it's that deviate from His plan. Meaning we can't see where we are going.

Our fall

We fall down but we get up
We listen to what is around
Lead by the unction as we are being stirred, your prayers have been
heard

We depend on the ONLY voice of Holy Spirit that teaches and
guides us
He is the revealer of Truth, just remember the story about Ruth
Although there are many sounds all around, we are not wavered or
distracted by it not even a little bit

We tap in the radio frequency of Heaven that has been produced
We are a product of Christ's first fruits
The fire didn't consume you
Why?
Because Jesus was in there too
All because He Loves you

Weeping may endure for a night, but joy comes in the morning light
We are living in the Glory of God
You are never far from His Heart
You have been crafted by His hands; Which is apart of His divine
plans

We walk by faith and not by sight
We worship and praise God; with All our might
God wishes to do you NO harm
Know that you safe in the Master's arm

Ornitha Danielle

We Just!

In a world with so many uncertainties, but knowing that God is
greater than those!

We can fiddle our thumbs about what this world will be,
No matter of all the sin around us, the killing and the many things
that
We don't see

We tend to run ourselves mad
We forget how to live; we forget how to laugh, and how to dance,
We just forget how to just literally BE!

Learning something new, isn't of the devil, listening to jazz isn't
dripping in the demonic realm, letting go and allow God to show you
how great living in His abundant live He gave you.

Your Next Destination

The things that you've had to learn, stop, move forward, turn away from, keep, toss away, hold tighter, smile at, cry about... Old seasons, nobody could've prepared you for the journey ahead, that journey was to lead you to your next destination.

Think about it, I love using the Wizard of Oz... Dorothy had taken a pretty good knot on her head, like we all have in life to point us in the right direction... running away from what God has already planned for your life is never what we want at times. I can admit honestly to that... Sometimes it's much easier to create our own paths, and God doesn't force us to choose Him, but it is He that chooses us for the road that lies ahead.

I sometimes wonder, if we ever would be given a glimpse of what that road ahead would be like. I know for me like our friend Dorothy would have made better choices, but I thank God for His grace and mercy along the way. His keeping me in the right state of mind while on the road. If we look back, we can see the individuals that she met while in search for what she had already at home. When we get a little irritation, immediately we want to do something different, especially when it comes to spiritual things, hello Danielle! I'd spent a lot of times messing up royally!

Oh, but there is a God, that cares about me! It's so strange how quickly we would turn to other people without taking the time to seek God FIRST! And those people can't are not even sure what direction they are going in, let alone tell you anything that can help you. The blind leading the blind.

As I am writing this it is evident that we as believers allow to many people give us advise, or is it that we already know what God is going to say or is it that we know what answer is going to be? We step out there and we need to form our own cheering section that will agree with our plans... We need to totally and honestly fallout of agreement with anything that exalts it's over what is right and pleasing to God.

Now, to me that movie The Wizard of Oz, is very prophetic all thought out... I will let you be the judge of that. Follow the yellow brick road.... the streets are paved with gold?

Okay, the point that I am trying to make, the deeper Dorothy went, the road became harder...and her friends were no better off than she was... the scarecrow said he didn't have a brain already, so clearly he couldn't make decision... the tin man, was very emotional... he was without a heart, which he was lead by his emotions or the lack thereof, and the lion... a bully and he stated his problem, but she still allow them to be her friends.

Another look at this, sometimes traveling a long is lonely, that we at times want people along no matter what condition that are in. it's so many twists and turns that I could take with my observation....

I myself don't entertain the idea, of any kind witch, and pixie dust, and magic... and potions, and of casting spells... it's real! It's crazy how much people will believe in the demonic side, but refuses to believe in the supernatural the Heavenly Kingdom?

The bible clearly speaks of evil, Satan feel from heaven... Going forward, we have to be careful who we allow to be our traveling friends, sometimes and most times there issues tend to become or issues... but I want to believe that later on, these friends truly got it together and was able to contend for her, when she was captured by the evil witch...

Fairytales' of Reality

Slowly she walked passed the hanging mirror afraid of the staring image that she sees, Thoughts of histories and time that has escaped pondering for now fate. Her hair, her smile, and her delicate poise as the glory of God's love illuminates the room, she glides across the floor as life awaits her at the door.

Movies and fairytales about undying love, or romanticizing, about what love is... to love or not to be loved is the aged old question that still remain. encased in the depth of her soul untamed

She stops and backs up again by the oblong shaped mirror that hangs effortlessly on the wall for another look, what is shown is a child in need of assurance and full of innocence, nothing left unturned or in despair

Cinderella is the fairest Bella of the ball, all dressed up with nowhere to go, she tries to move forward, but her feet are planted firmly to the floor, that time and space, she tries to run and hide, but reality is that, it can't be, or is it an illusion of a fairytale illustrated on paper, of a colorful childlike imagination playing in the playgrounds or falling aimlessly as the stars in the skies dangling before her eyes.

Broken down into the smallest form known possible... Handled with care by angelic host sent on assignment to help her in life's journey. Close the door, or play the cards that you are dealt, win loose or draw or let's make a deal? Too many things to think about as she critiques her realities based on Fairytale dreams, or could this be another dream, waiting to be panned out on wide-screen.

Take one, take two... Stage left is opening to exit the dream, or Break a leg, or time for makeup, where's the director for this scene, she needs to tell them, just what she has seen.

Stage coaches, horses and mice to help pull of the figment of what she dreamed, visions of purple hearts, green clovers and blue diamonds, to the rabbit who's always late. Late you do say? Tricks are for kids, eat your Wheaties and grow big and strong, drink this and you will shrink again, or eat this, a rich sweet taste that you can't resist. Off to dreamland again... asleep waiting on the one that can intercede for her, or will it be hit or miss?

The kingdom of this world has fallen under demise of the enemy's plan to conquer the Empire of the souls of people that has drifted off to some foreign land, in exchange for happiness

In that mirror was a door, or realm of mysteries unknown.... looking forward to be that child claimed as their own, but yet in a world of uncertainties are just our true realities?

Fairytales are very entertaining by the least, mind wondering of the love affair between the beauty and beast? Unchartered love, unnatural in every way... to the Prince charming to awaken Sleeping Beauty with a simple kiss upon her lips, which becomes the antidote to break the spell of darkness over her life

Taking a ride on the magic carpet, to see beyond ones own eye, to rubbing a jar and making a wish? Supernatural experience of God's grace, His guidance into his presence...

Fairytales of reality. Reality is that fairytales are what they are deceptive devices to plaque the minds and imaginations of the innocence and youth. Reality is that God's love never gets old; He's the true lover of our souls.

Uncertainties

Pondering thoughts of what seems to be a fairytale of the sea,
1000 feet below,
Is a dark mystery?
Honestly just between you and me, lies are what they be! Interesting
enough you heard that correctly, twists, turns, and whatever else you
believe, what matters now is God's truth, so hold on to your seat as
we are on a classic voyage

The race to the finish line? I'm late, says the rabbit, late for what,
more lies and the truth be told a line from the famous story of
wonderland of Alice
For what you may ask, speaking of that, as a matter of fact... the
space between happiness and devastation is what lies beneath

Riddle in a fantasy world of the simple games that are played
And we call them
Innocent child's play
Your turn, my turn, all around the mulberry bush, for what?
To join in a ring around the roses, until they all fall down
London Bridges?
Real truth about the lies in nursery rhythms
Lies that we memorized in infancy to whisper in the delicate ears of
the listener
To repeat a cycle of chaos to be passed on to generation after
generation?

Potions and spells again more lies that God has already unveiled,
dismantle by His strong hand
Magic, white spells or little lies.... it's still a lie in the believer's eye.
Come closer, there is more to tell the enemy is coning,
Don't you see?

There's nothing more wrong in any of this foolery can't you see?
Salvation is truth, for our everlasting ending!
Religion, tradition and legalism that keeps the body moving forward
to fulfill the purpose and the destiny that God wrote write with his

finger, concerning us! Anything other than God's plans, which were a good work, create by his hands, the best master plan.

Tricking and plotting is what the enemy does, all throughout history we can see, as we travel down memory lane, stories that where told to scare and poison the innocent mind.
Why do you ask?
To through off the plans of what God had in mind, to give you and I life so divine.

Hush little baby, don't say a word even more secrets, the cycle must stop!
We've silenced the young, to speak, when the familiarities of spirits have entered into terrorizing them over and over again, this wasn't God's plan.
It was the enemy of our soul,
who lost his place and he's just mad

Classic stories that we know all too well, of horror and disbelief that plague our minds.
When things spiritual and divine of the things that Christ did, it's dismissed with unbelief
Let's back up for a moment,
Spiritual of Kingdom living, we can't believe, but we are intrigued by powers of darkness easily?

My friends remember fairytales about the tooth fairy, who was to come and take your tooth and leave you money for it? All too well, we've bought into the plans of darkness and the cycle begins to repeat it. Let's stop now and because our enemy has been defeated.

Never Forfeit

Never forfeit the calling or the promises of God to satisfy flesh or man. Today stand for righteous and holiness. Intimacy with the Lord is where you come to know more about Him and His character, and who you are in Him. Pursue God, more than your own will. What is your message, does it speak the opposite of what you actually do? The enemy knows who Jesus is and he knows who we are too.

Develop your own prayer muscle, by spending time in His presence, along with eating the written word of God, will begin to shift and remove the surface things that have been taught to many of us down through the years. This season of where we are is about to blow the lid off of religious mindset, traditional and denominational.

Levels & Stages of Healing

There are levels and stages of healing that has to take place in a person's life that has suffered from a traumatic trauma somewhere in life. It could come from a number of factors. Lost of a love one

Placing a bandage over the wound is only a temporary fix. The moment something happens to cause a person to re-live that time in their life... that wound starts to ooze again, attitudes starts flaring and things are said in the heat of the moment causing more wounding.

It really does take time to heal from whatever that issue is. Sometimes it takes people a little longer to get through it... and now they have to process it again, then release but only with God's help. God never forces again, unlike man. Oftentimes man feels and think a person should've gotten over an issue even if it was 10, 20, or 30 years ago... it could very well be longer...

The point I am making here is... There's a lot of people right now in the body of Christ are going through this very thing. They love God; serve in many facets of ministries, and more that are still wounded. Getting to the matter at hand and going through a healing process, which is learning to forgive and understand that God has forgiven you... that was an act that was displayed on the cross for ALL humanity!

Journaling Through The Process

Journaling Through the process.... Allow God to deal with you. Sometimes we have to have a place to put things.... our thoughts, our emotions, our hopes, dreams and desires.

There's a need to look at where we've been so that we can find out where we're going. God wants to create a new you, with less traumatic and pressing issues, which keep us hiding behind the walls of guilt, anger and pain.

I'm sure that there are many other things that are just simply floating around in our minds. That when it comes up, we shrink back. It's time to face it, God wants to restore everything that enemy has stolen from us illegally.

God's Plan

I have to salute my hubby this morning as I do everyday for being the man of God that which God knew I needed. It's really amazing how he's been my **BIGGEST SUPPORTER IN EVERYTHING!** He's been there through thick and thin... as back in the day the would say I would say you go, I go, Imma ridin' witcha no matter what. He's really a man of very few words, well until he gets to know you.

He watches and listens to **EVERYTHING**! I say we've gone to the ends of the earth riding on nothing but pure fumes of life. If nobody in the understand me, he does!

People can say that they understand what going through the storm, marriage takes real work, and that's on both parts. Sometimes I laugh at the stuff we did very early in our relationship... Two imperfect souls, with not a clue in the world what we were getting into.... This was truly God's plan from the beginning of creation. When we talk about how God orchestrated our meeting... it's a storybook romance for real.

I'll never forget the day we meet, and I am still blushing. There's no book that can tell you how to be a husband, a father, nor a mother, or a wife... you kind of have to learn that on your own... I just want to encourage you today.... no matter what it looks like or what other people say, know that God is the best antidote to life's problem.

What He Requires?

God is God all by himself. I never or understood, by before how the spirit of competition has wounded so many of God's people even myself included. I have spent the past few years studying in the Apostolic Prophetic School of The Scribe, which has brought forth so much healing, restoration and understanding in my life as a Scribe as well as God's Scribal Prophet.

It's not weird that Holy Spirit who dwells down on the inside of you will start to arise and stand against those very things that exalts itself above God. It's not weird that a Scribe finds himself or herself moving in different realms and dimensions under the Scribal Anointing! It's not weird that you have an urgency to produce that play, or that poem, or write that book, or even paint, sometimes all at once in a course of a day.

I am a vessel that has been commissioned, and assigned for a time such as this to make God's name know in the earth. I'm not just a prophetic minister that moves in movement way of God's leading. See as many, many see it or might even say; oh she's just a dancer? There's more to that, and more to God's spirit. I'm pulling down strongholds, depression, standing face to face with the enemy at times contending for those that may not have the ability to do on their own.

There's been considerable amount of growth in my understanding. I'm forever thankful that I don't operate out of a religious mindset at this moment in life. I know what God requires, and to see how what I even thought at one time to be God pulled the scales from my eyes.

Ornitha Danielle

War Silently

I had this dream not like anyone that I have ever had before. I had me almost afraid to move.... oh but God! I knew something wasn't right from the beginning. Glory! I can't fight, the Apostolic Prophetic on my life, I war silently!!! I wait until I have clarity and when God shifts I go with God.

As I was in the midst of the dream realm. Silk appeared to me... she started out okay, but she quickly hanged! It was some demonic snake. It began to contort. Immediately fear rose in me.... I was backed up into a corner.... first thing I thought was to grab my belt and she said. What's in me likes that. She had a bony type of back; you could see the bones of it... I went back to a child's place where fear rose up in me... I completely had forgotten how to pray.... I ran to my mom's room, slamming the door, but she was very strong.

Then I noticed two doors together on the bedroom? I locked them both. Without ever opening. I reached for baby oil and put all round the door. And under the door, and then all of sudden it got vicious. I asked my for something, she said open the door so she could see... I said I am not doing that! She uses the oil/lotion that she got from some ministry event. I remember getting that and using it.... I woke up in prayer. I am still trembling; I stood toe to toe... I get it.

Un-Blurred Vision

I try not to get caught up in world trends and saying who's right or
wrong. I for one read, study and understands of what scripture has to
say, only JESUS CHRIST IS THE ONLY WAY!
Keeping my eyes open, mind spirit clear, and my ear as close to the
heart of God
I wait and listen as HE speaks to my heart
Praying and trying to walk in the destiny and purpose that
God created just for me
Warnings, directions, encouragement and everything in between
I promise sometimes it can be too much too see,
The stillness and unbelievable things that are revealed of what I see
in the midst of my dream

Such a photographic memory,
Its like I'm watching a movie on widescreen!
With angelic instructions of what I am to do, as I wait, I watch, and I
listen to the mysteries that only God can bring
I remember when I started my Scribal journey, understanding what
that really meant
Knowing what I know, wow, that was sometime far spent.
That day, He'd been preparing me for the roads ahead, each day God
continues to walk closely with me. I'm the one that asks Tons of
questions, but I do a lot of watching instead at the phase in my
journey.

As, Apostle John, stated that he was caught up in the spirit on the
Lord's Day. I myself beheld a vision of scrolls that were descending
from heaven, they were trails of books with angel wings, as far as I
could see, and they were books that where written by me
I didn't understand at first, but now I do

Abba Father, you reign so mighty with the stroke of my pen, and
blood ink that drips from its tip... to scribe out what you would have
me say.
**My God I write what you say and honor the authority of my pen that
you gave me.**

Wake Up

The thought of the vivid winds on face as my heart beats and entered
the love race
As I turned around to the invisible and to the enviable things that
piqued my interest
Inquisitive of the sound waves that are my length of processing the
supernatural things
The vision of angelic wings
He is who knows all, and desire that I seek him now, while He can
still be found
Streams of songs, poems, and stories to reveal and bring Him Glory
Pen in hand these words begin to dance, one step, two step, kick ball
change
He is my king who still and forever reigns

The ink that spills from the fountain of my pen
These words flow as a prophetic wind
Shifting into dimensions, remember there's no glitch in the kingdom
system
Of God's Governmental System
No time to delay, Jesus Christ is the ONLY WAY
Trust Him and He'll see you through

Tick-tock, the sounding of the clock
There's nothing that should stop you from completing what has been
placed inside of you
Take heed now, He will carry and see you through

Reality Based Talk

Chances are that many will not take the time to thank God for making it to see yet another day. When He is the reason that your eyes opened, to view the Sun in the morning sky.

But rush to the television set to see when their favorite team will play, or to gather those lottery tickets in hopes of hitting it big soon one day, after scratching off that silver thin layer of pixie glaze, that will reveal that mystery number that somehow has been concealed. While grabbing for the key or coin and frantically on pins and needles hoping for that jackpot... money not well spent, down the drain it went... now the joke is on you. Rent, car note are due? Trying to see if you can a quick cash loan?

Don't mind my approach to the world that we live in. rush to get it, get in and get it now... my heart pumps fast as I think about times pass of those that are no longer here now... not just in body isn't what I speak about so have no fear, but that undeniable spirit of love in which my master talks about, so give him your ear.

You call on all the names above all names, before those that many pretend to be all-deep with, be careful now, the removal and the uncovering what's under the sheets. Believe it or not it's really like that? Who are you playing with? You must remember that He is the one who sees, knows and hears all...

As a matter of fact it's really is just like that, hour by hour, minute by minute we need to stop with the appearance of what looks like ministry, instead in reality it made for TV, glitz, fame and cheap champagne. Not having the Love of God, walking around with rotten and deep hatred for your brother, sister, Father and mother. Praying all cute, prophesying all deep, wanting to lay hands on everything that you see. Yet the heart is colder than the below freezing point. Riddle with hatred, lies and deceit this is called the modern day of sickness and disease. The number killer of the human race is UNFORGIVINESS, unfortunately next to its bitterness. Why so bold and harsh, I heard, but if you are living in His word then these things will never come near you... Just live in Truth!

Look don't take my word for it... if you can look at that image in the mirror and not feel a thing or see a reflection, chances are that what you see is the Walking dead looking to be restored, God can do just that if you will allow Him to, because my friend He died for you.

God is a healer, deliverer and His word said that He came for the sick. Sick in mind, body and spirit. It's a different type of power, none of this boss type of mentality, or being on a grown man or grown woman grind...

Broken in need of repair... God answers even in despair... Applauding those that are headed for demise? I'm confused I must say… clapping and singing them praises for their GENIUS? A machine that doesn't care of the age or gender it this world system that destroys God's people like a human blender.

Spiritual Prostitution

Up early this morning, as I was just talking to the Lord... Just really concerned about God's people and where we are... With so much, going on in the world around us.

As I was mediating on His word... I heard this... Prostitution is illegal in the natural; we have to come to terms that in the spiritual realm that it also applies. Think about it... ***Spiritual prostitution.***

The very things that God gives us, we have to protect it all cost. So many in the world have become spiritual prostitutes... I wasn't really sure what to actually do with that word. So I went to the dictionary and I looked it up, in doing so the Whoredom stood out (Whoredom) prostitution or other promiscuous sexual activity...

Generally we've come accustom to a woman in this category operating in sexual manners. However, it also applies to men as well. We have to stop treating Holy Spirit like a pimp... There was a covenant that God had made with the Children of Israel, but the children of Israel breached the contract... but falling out of love with their God, but ran after another who suited their own earthly and flesh desires.

Now I would like to switch your thoughts for a moment. Spiritual Prostitution what does that mean and look like in the life of a believer? We tend to worship God when it's convenient... not everyone, however we've become guilty at some point.

Many believers don't even realize that they are in this place. I want to lay a foundation for this teaching...

A person who misuses their talents or who sacrifices their self-respect for the sake of personal or financial gain is heading for trouble. (Gomar I am sure was very attractive) Prostitution and Whoredom can be used interchangeably...

Merriam - Webster dictionary.com defines the word Whoredom as:

1. The practice of whoring: prostitution
2. Faithless, unworthy, or idolatrous practices or pursuits

Prostitution
1: the work of a prostitute: the act of having sex in exchange for money
2. The use of a skill or ability in a way that is not appropriate or respectable

Debased
1: to lower the value or reputation of (someone or something) to make (someone or something) less respected

So immediately as was preparing this message, I asked the Lord, what would He have for me to feed His people? Immediately the Lord reminded me of Prophet Hosea and Gomar.

Hosea 1:2
When the Lord first spoke through Hosea, the Lord said to him, "Go, take for yourself a wife of prostitution and have children of her prostitution; for the land commits great acts of prostitution by not following the Lord." As, God instructed and told Prophet Hosea to marry a prostitute for a reason. That's not everyone's story nor journey, but those that are to walk in this WILL BE EQUIPPED FOR IT!

Hosea 2
Here the Lord has Hosea to speak to His people and to explain how it had been Him providing for them, but what He provided they gave to their god Baal for idol worship verse worshipping the true and living God.

Can you see this playing out? Here scripture explains to us that, they forgot their first love.

That was the typical response. My people are exploiting themselves for the cares of this world. Now I am thinking. It's not just those in high places, this is right in the body of Christ!

Remembrance

I so love when Holy Spirit reminds you of your journey when the shift changed in your life for the better. I know I may have shared this before, I can't ever take credit or for granted of what God is doing in my life and at this point in the ministry that he gave me.

I use to try and explain who I was and why I did the things that I did. But when God begins to shift your perspective on the things around you. You can't be good at something if you don't put the time and effort into it. God gave each and everyone talents, which takes me to story of the man with the 5 talents over in the book of Matthew. We are to develop what has been placed in our hands, but at times we don't always know what to do with those things and we bury them never to be seen again.

My thought quickly went to this, when God gives each of us, we have to develop it. Gifts and callings are irrevocable. Whether or not a person decides to come in relation with God, but you are still responsible for it. But if we become slothful and disobedient to the calling upon our lives we can delay our journey, we spend more time on the road, and that can produce frustration in our walks.

What He's given you; He can easily take it away and give it to another. One there will come a time when to make good on that investment. Have something in your reserve where you can withdraw when needed.

Daniel The Influencer

Daniel and the 3 Hebrew boys... we're indeed gifted spiritually and naturally in their teens. King Nebecukezzar knew this prior to that capture. I believe that they had also been spying on these before hand.

Holy spirit revealed that in this new season that we'll have to depend on him when He places us in places to begin to prophesy. To foretell of the inner workings in God's people and how they operate. As Daniel and the three Hebrew boys, plead their case to the eunuch who had really grown very fond of him in regards to the meal.

That too rose a bit of questioning with the king. When I was mediating I got to thinking. Then the Lord said.... your gift will bring you before the great, but this is what should and must happen while you are there.

Where I am not known, you must see to it that I am. Be not afraid for I am with you. What I have placed in your mouth and in you will amaze many, that will cause them to question what they once thought, and many will come to know me.

Each time, Daniel was given knowledge to mysteries that only God in heaven could reveal. The king didn't remember, so he couldn't explain or tell what he saw.... Daniel went and sought the Lord. Then God opened that realm of the King's dream and gave interpretation. However, I am convinced that the king wasn't fully understanding of the interpretation that he did just what the dream revealed each time.

Sadly, my spirit believes Daniel desired to leave... begin away from his home and family... He was set over kingdom as well as serving in several kingships. I have to say as a influencer for God's kingdom more and more people saw, knew, and understood that God's kingdom is forever and He's all knowing and all seeing and all powerful. I maybe jumping a bit... excitement.... Daniel was a faith and loyal to God, and couldn't be swayed no other way.

He was willing along with the 3 Hebrew boys... I will lay down my life for it, at young ages. As we look back over the punishment that the faced at the king or those in leadership... but God is a vindicator. Who couldn't or wouldn't want to serve a God like that. Each time I read or go over the story again.

The visions and dreams are becoming more increasingly heightened in this new shift. The Apostolic and prophetic thrust is upon the land. We're going to have to truly rely on Holy Spirit to show us everything.... king Darius was actually interceding on behalf of Daniel while he was in the lion's den.

Stop It and Use Wisdom

Had it ever occurred that sometimes healing and deliverance should be in a safe and private environment? There are stages of this, and it shouldn't display like I have seen in some of these videos circling around the Internet and social media.

We must use wisdom, to prevent more injury. Looking at the life of Job, look at the friends that were around him. It was when Job was alone.... crying out to God. Look at David, the death of his child.... even the circumstances sounding it... we can look at Hagar... she had an encounter with the angel of the Lord, so did Jacob, when he wrestled with the angel. Not everything is needed for public display, but the results of it will be witnessed.

Too many times when people are looking for breakthroughs, it's a very emotional time and sensitive in nature and therefore we mustn't be careless with God's people. Screaming and yelling; all in the microphones prophesying, what is believed that the Lord is saying.

Wisdom! Wisdom! I can't stress it enough. I do believe in encouragement and edification, but sometimes it should be done in private as well, or in the safety of accountability. Someone that can test the words... when you have worshipped, prayed and study with a person you knows them by the spirit.

I'm not talking about no spirit of familiarity... this is another issue of mine as well. I get so sick and tired of some believers have taken a position of I can do this and that and a third, and still get up and preach, sing, shout and minister unto the Lord. Gifts and callings are without repentance!

Operating out or on gifting, but lack the anointing. We can just simply allow this foolery to go on, causing others to stumble and fall... We've just stepped into a place of compromise in what we believe and know is right? We can't come into agreement with such practices.... we are to love, but not to align ourselves with that, anything less than what God has for us.

Next Phase

In this section of this book, here's an opportunity for you to get pen and paper and do an outline to the next phase in life and on your journey. Begin writing down your goals, short and long term. Where do you plan on going and what would you like to do?

Where we are in this season, it's going to require more than the surface stuff to get us through the next phase in our journey. You are going to have to bring your A game, and prepare to battle in the spirit.

You're going to need your weapons in order to engage in spiritual warfare... and understanding the difference of what to use for certain battles. Spiritual strategic planning and spiritual mapping, of when, how, what and where you should execute your spiritual move. Develop your spiritual compass for your direction. Make this a daily routine in your life and refer back to this from time to time. With determination and God as your pilot you can achieve those things that you write about. My prayer is with you as you travel to your next phase and journey in life.... What's on your road map?

About The Author

Ornitha Danielle is the proud mother of three children, grandmother of one and the wife to Rodney 'Lee' Taylor whom is a professional freelance photographer. She resides in Memphis, TN., where she writes full-time and pursuing her dreams as a Christian Author, teacher (Master **SCRIBE, His Scribal Prophet**) Blogger, Editor-in-Chief of So Fyh Magazine Online, Poet, Educator, Minister, Prophetic Liturgical Praise Worshipper, and an Inspirational/ Motivational Speaker. She uses the authority of her pen to share personal and practical issues that can help others overcome the harsh reality of life and learning how to cope.

In her former career she was a professional hairstylist and makeup artist, which allowed her to be chic, unique and edgy and yet very creative without boundaries. With the many things that God has placed in your hands, she's able to move freely in Him.

Ornitha Danielle is truly God's (His Scribal Prophet). She's reached beyond the surface and extended her eagle's wings and soared further than the clouds and became an educator in her field of expertise and taught in several beauty schools in the Memphis area. Not much she later became a salon owner of *Perfection of Beauty*, after working many years as a Master Stylist for a well know franchise she decided to return to school.

After graduating from Southwest Tennessee Community College, it opened a very different perspective on one of her many loves, which happens to be the love of writing. Her grasp of the love for words, and freedom of written expression, her craft of creative writing has allowed this novelist to venture into a new marketplace and create that path for her unique style of writing. Ornitha Danielle is pursued a specialty in Media Communications at Full Sail University.

As fulltime freelance journalist for many publications which one being the Tri-State Defender Newspaper in Memphis, TN and many other publications including her own online magazine So Fyh Magazine Online. She's a successful online radio personality, for "Let's Talk Literary with Ornitha Danielle and a media journalist for Black Butterfly Media TV. She also a National Media Director for Voices of Christ Literary Ministries International, as well as the visionary of Souls Ignited International Ministries.

This new area in life, career businesswoman, and ministry in motion has found its home in Literary Ministry. Ornitha Danielle is currently working to obtain her Associate of Applied Sciences degree in Allied Health Science, and working on many other projects as well as penning her next book.

Ornitha Danielle